NO MERE IRISH:
THE KENNEDYS OF MOUNT KENNEDY

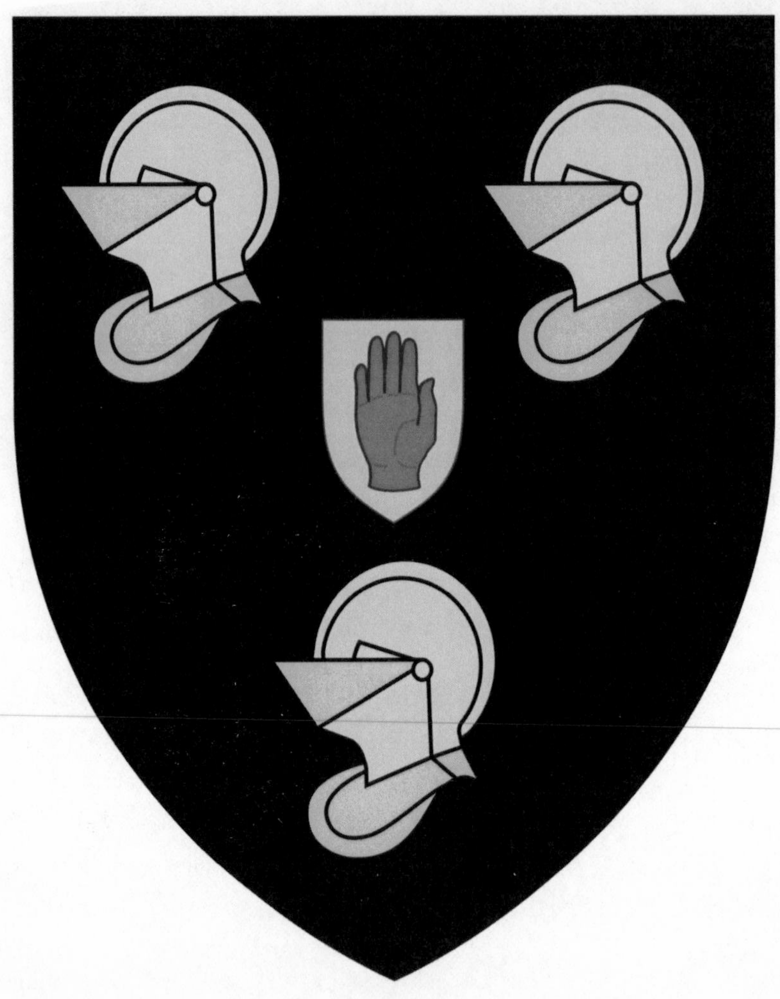

Coat of Arms awarded to Robert Kennedy in 1619, originally with a scallop shell, amended to the red hand, mark of a baronet in1664.

NO MERE IRISH:
THE KENNEDYS OF MOUNT KENNEDY

Therese Hicks

Wordwell

First published by Wordwell Ltd, 2022
Dublin, Ireland

www.wordwellbooks.com

First Edition

Wordwell is an imprint of the Wordwell Group

The Wordwell Group
Unit 9, 78 Furze Road
Sandyford
Dublin, Ireland

Print ISBN: 978-1-913934-76-7
Ebook ISBN: 978-1-913934-80-4

British Library Cataloguing in Publication Data.
A catalogue record for this book is available from the British Library.

Typeset in ITC New Baskerville by Wordwell Ltd, Dublin.

Copy-editor: Emer Condit

Cover design and artwork: Ronan Colgan

Printed by: Sprint Print, Dublin

Contents

Acknowledgements

My journey to this book began with a suggestion from Chris Corlett of the NMS that I should look into the history of the Kilmurry church ruins, just west of Newtownmountkennedy. I would often visit this place on my local walks. That suggestion led me to search for the estate papers of Mount Kennedy in the hope of discovering some information on the building. Because the second major owner of Mount Kennedy, Gen. Robert Cunningham, had been made Lord Rossmore, I first pursued the Rossmore Papers, hoping that the Kennedy papers would be with them. Lord Rossmore had been childless and, on his death, his title, along with the Rossmore Papers, went to his wife's people in Monaghan.

This led me to a phone conversation with Enda Galligan, a local historian in that county. It was he who was able to tell me that the Mount Kennedy estate papers were to be found in the Wicklow Papers, which reside in the National Library of Ireland (NLI). Only for that piece of great good luck, I may never have found them, as there is no reference to them in the introduction to the catalogue of the Wicklow Papers. My experience of luck soon turned to despair, however, when I first held one of these documents in my hand. They are written in the English secretary hand, an eyeball twisting forerunner to our current approach to letter formation.

Coincidentally, I had, at that time, started attending the Mícheál Ó Cléirigh lectures at University College Dublin (UCD). Caught between my despair and my determination to unlock the information in the estate papers, I asked John McCafferty if he knew of any graduate students who would be willing to help me learn how to read it. He suggested Jeffrey Cox, whom I duly contacted. Jeffrey was extremely generous with his time, spending two and a half days side by side with me at the NLI, helping me to get my eye on the script. He also suggested online sites for attaining this skill. After that, it took two and a half years of slogging before I had transcribed the 450 or so relevant documents.

Transcribing documents is only half the battle, however. Learning the context of their composition is extremely important. For this I needed to talk to the experts, who have been exceedingly generous with their time and knowledge. Initially, Kenneth Nicholls, whose familiarity with the relevant topics is extensive and detailed, directed my research. He had dealt with the Kennedy papers before they were catalogued in his pursuit of the O'Byrnes. He critiqued my early drafts which enabled me to pass a peer review.

From there Raymond Gillespie continued to expand my research, helping me to identify my many assumptions about the seventeenth century which were leading me astray. A number of drafts ensued, continually honing and expanding my understanding of the Kennedys and their world. The final draft was critiqued by both Kenneth and Raymond, each drawing on their immense knowledge of the people and times covered in this book.

Others who have made contributions are: Colin Armstrong, David Brown, Mary Clarke, Howard Clarke, Mark Clinton, Coleman Dennehy, Mark Empey, Alan Ford, Rob Goodbody, Aideen Ireland, Stuart Kinsella, Colm Lennon, Con Manning, Hazel Maynard, John McCafferty, Brid McGrath, Ivar McGrath, John Medlycott, Elinor Nuttall Medlycott, Caren Mulcahy, Frances Nolan, Tim O'Neill, Liam O'Rourke, Geoffrey Scott OSB, Paul Smith, Ciaran Wallace, Brian Hollinshead of Open Street Mapping for the map of the estate's townlands, Mary Kelly for help in the translation of the Latin texts, Pat Reid of the Heritage Council, and Conchubhar Ó Crualaoich of the Placenames Commission. The staffs of the NLI, National Archives of Ireland (NAI), Dublin City Library and Archives (DCLA), Trinity College Library, the Royal Irish Academy library, Marsh's Library, Greystones Library, the Wicklow Local Studies Library, Office of the Chief Herald, and the Kildare Historical Society have also been very helpful, facilitating my pursuit of sources and details. The Robert Kennedy coat of arms and editing of the signatures were generously contributed by Jonathan Tallon of Good Ideas, jon@goodideas.ie.

With this huge amount of assistance, the text has taken shape. The usual caveat holds true, of course — all mistakes are my own.

Abbreviations

ARD	*Calendar of Ancient Records of Dublin*
CPR	*Calendar of the Patent Rolls James I*
CPCR	*Calendar of the patent and close rolls of Chancery in Ireland, of the reign of Charles I*
CSPI	*Calendar of State Papers relating to Ireland*
DCLA	Dublin City Library and Archives
DIB	*Dictionary of Irish Biography*
DNB	*Dictionary of National Biography*
JRSAI	*Journal of the Royal Society of Antiquaries of Ireland*
NAI	National Archives of Ireland
NLI	National Library of Ireland
NMS	National Monument Service of Ireland
PRONI	Public Record Office of Northern Ireland
RCB	Representative Church Body, Church of Ireland
TNA	The National Archives of the UK

Note on dates

In seventeenth-century England and Ireland, the number of the year did not change until 25 March. Thus, dates between 1 January and 24 March were still written as being of the previous year from a modern point of view. Therefore, all dates that fall within these months in this book are written in a hybrid form, e.g., 1624/25. Pope Gregory instituted a correction, which became known as the Gregorian calendar, which the West still follows today. Protestant countries refused to accept this change until well into the eighteenth century.

List of illustrations

Introduction

The Kennedys of Mount Kennedy were an ambitious seventeenth-century Irish family of Gaelic background who were remarkable for having emerged from obscurity at the beginning of a tumultuous century and for achieving a significant level of success on the wider stage. Initially based in Dublin, and probably related to a wealthy merchant branch of Dublin Kennedys, they built a wide-ranging network of contacts and gained court offices, which allowed them to amass wealth and establish a manor in County Wicklow. This is in noticeable contrast to the many Gaelic families whose prestige and landholdings sharply declined throughout this century, especially in the aftermath of the 1641 rebellion and the Cromwellian decade of the 1650s.[1]

Their achievement in having not only survived but also thrived before and after the restoration of the monarchy in 1660 provides us with a story that takes us through this entire century at the level of a middle-ranking family. For strategic reasons they had become Protestant, most probably in the late 1590s, and threw in their lot with the New English adventurers and settlers. We are able to follow Irish history from their point of view as they navigate the shift from the dominance of Anglo-Norman Catholic families to the acquisition of vast tracts of land by New English Protestants, along with the latter's emerging control of the government.

As has been explained elsewhere,[2] the transfer of huge areas of Ireland to new owners in the late sixteenth and early seventeenth centuries could not have been carried out without the co-operation of many enablers within the system of the courts and other government branches. These greasers of wheels gained substantially in the process, not just for their services but also for their understanding of *how* it was done. Others would pay handsomely for such knowledge and advice.

This book will delineate the route taken by this Kennedy family, who have otherwise been forgotten with the passage of time.

Much of their story is to be found in the Mount Kennedy estate papers, which only came into public ownership in the 1950s when the Earls of Wicklow, the Howards of Shelton Abbey, donated their papers to the National Library of Ireland. A marriage between the Kennedys and the Howards in the early 1680s saw the eventual inclusion of Kennedy documents in this much larger set; it is unlikely that they would otherwise have survived. There are roughly 450 documents pertaining to this Kennedy family in varying states of preservation, written on vellum and paper.

The documents are primarily legal contracts relating to property transactions, in both Dublin and Wicklow, from the mid-sixteenth to the mid-eighteenth century. They are indentures of sale with related 'articles of agreement', rental agreements, wills and court cases. In addition, there are obligations (promissory notes), personal letters, marriage contracts, receipts and some financial accounts from the late seventeenth century. Of the entire corpus, about two dozen of the documents had previously been typed (and appear as such in the collection). Some of these are duplicates of surviving originals, while others preserve material that is now lost (see Illus. 1).

There are, however, noticeable gaps in the estate papers. Some of these are probably due to lack of attention in filing them away or later scatterings, and some that survived outside the collection up to the second decade of our current century have been lost through carelessness,[3] but other factors, such as decisions that some documents were no longer worth saving (especially documents witnessing short-term transactions), will skew to some extent our picture of what was happening over the years. Even those that survive give us no insight into any kind of overall planning that may have been conceived of for a longer-term goal.

In addition to the estate papers, there are other sources that tell us something about this family. These include the State Papers, the Patent Rolls of James I, the Report of the Irish Commission of 1622, the Down Survey, the Calendar of Inquisitions, the 1641 Depositions, a Claim before Commissioners of Revenue in Dublin (1653), the documents of the Restoration Land Settlement, and records of Trinity College, Lincoln's Inn, the Royal Archives and the archives of the English Benedictines at Douai Abbey, among others. From these we get a much more complete picture of the family's early manoeuvrings, their

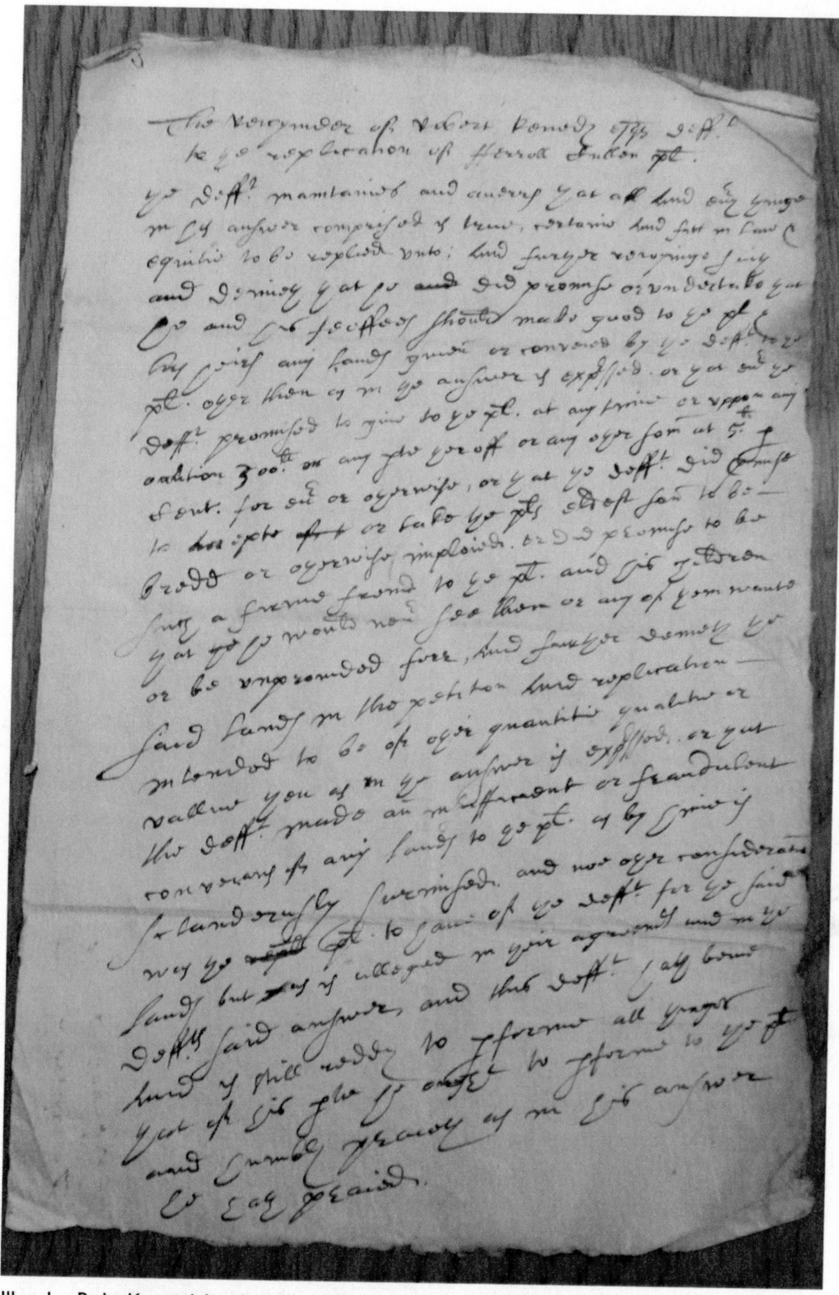

Illus. 1—Robt Kennedy's rebuttal to Farrell O'Cullen's charges, written in his own hand.

ongoing strategies for expansion and self-preservation, later developments and, ultimately, these Kennedys' demise.

Since documentation of landownership was extremely important in this century, the family saved many documents from the sixteenth and early seventeenth centuries concerning property which they would later own. Some of these include legal interactions between the Gaelic property-holders of north County Wicklow, thus providing insight into land and money transactions among a group whose records rarely survive at this level. In addition, there are legal exchanges between the Kennedys and local families such as the O'Cullens and the O'Byrnes, detailing promises which the head of this family, Robert Kennedy, is said to have made to them, inducing them to seek mortgages from him.

In the seventeenth century there were different ways to gain wealth as opposed to maintaining or enlarging one's already accumulated wealth. Richard Boyle is the prime example of how someone from an initially landless state could rise to great wealth and power, he having become the first Earl of Cork. He did this primarily by manipulating the government's administrative system, making it serve himself rather than the Crown. Networks at this level could involve other government employees, and sometimes the middle management layer.[4]

For those who already possessed considerable land and were among the local élite, it was necessary to cultivate political connections at the highest levels. The Earls of Clanricard and Thomond would be obvious examples here.[5] It was their relationships with the king and his courtiers that allowed them to consolidate their holdings and protect them from various legal threats. They were effective players within aristocratic English circles. There were also those Gaelic landowners who fully embraced the legal approach to landownership in English titles, exemplified by the O'Ferralls of Longford.[6] The Kennedys have much more in common with Richard Boyle than with this second set of property-owners, as they originally did not own property.

The other important factor in the late sixteenth and early seventeenth centuries was religion. While the Crown's position was gradually becoming firmer against Catholics, people themselves held a variety of stances across a spectrum. At one end there were the hard-line Catholics who would tolerate no compromise. Then there were the flexible Catholics, who were willing to go along to get along. Fairly middle of the road theologically was the Established Church, which under James I and Charles I wanted to be as accommodating as possible to Catholics, within limits. They disliked hard-liners of both stripes. Moving on, there were reforming Protestants, who felt that the Established Church hadn't gone far enough in adopting the doctrinal and liturgical changes of the Continental reformers such as Luther and Calvin. At the other end of the spectrum were the radical Protestants, some known as Puritans. They also brooked no compromise and considered the rest ungodly. We will see that life on the ground in terms of religion was not black and white, and strange bedfellows could sometimes be found.

Because this family was primarily 'of the Cittie of Dublin', it is helpful to understand the place in which they lived and worked. J.T. Gilbert's *The History of the City of Dublin* can give us a better grasp of it in those days. Writing in the mid-1860s, and not long after the work of the Wide Street Commissioners had transformed the city, Gilbert had collected, one by one, what each street looked like, who lived there and what they got up to. Dublin in the seventeenth century was a noticeably different place than it is today. Before the Commissioners had done away with much of its medieval character, Dublin was a warren of narrow lanes, often overhung by houses that expanded out over the street with each additional storey. This would have restricted the amount of light from above. Although the city walls were often in poor repair, they still separated it from its suburbs, with access limited to gates at useful points. Relative to what we experience today, it was a much smaller place, measured in hundreds of feet from the central market cross to any city gate. Speed's map of 1610 (Illus. 2) provides us with an understanding of its layout. (See also Appendix B.)

The wider context

Historians refer to the period from 1550 to 1700 as the 'early modern'. It is the time of transition between a medieval mind-set and a modern one. The medieval mind was centred on the Christian faith as understood by the Latin Roman Catholic authorities. Initially, Latin had been the language of communication across the western Roman Empire. All literate people would have been educated in it, and many local people would probably have understood it. Early on, the original Greek New Testament and the Septuagint (the Greek translation of the Hebrew Old Testament) had been translated into Latin. Readings from it were understandable by many, as were the prayers of the Mass

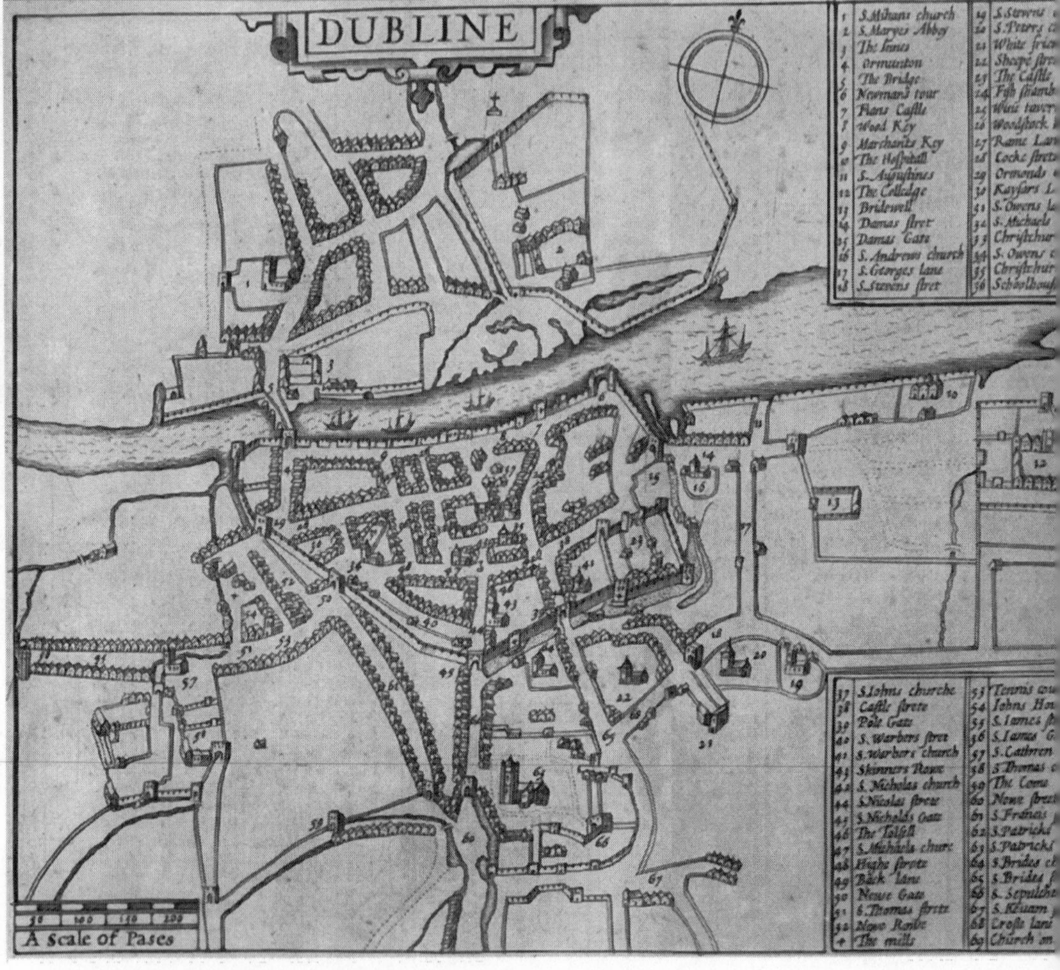

Illus. 2—Speed's 1610 map of Dublin, with key opposite (from H.B. Clarke, *Irish Historic Towns Atlas No. 11: Dublin, Part I, to 1610* (Dublin, 2002); used with permission).

(though, of course, forms of Greek would have continued to be used in the eastern Mediterranean).

As time wore on, however, local vernaculars replaced Latin, and only the educated could understand these basic documents and rituals of the Christian religion. Religious services became very mysterious, awe-inspiring and theatrical. They spoke to people through their senses rather than through their intellect. In addition, the many practices of pre-Christian European religions, which were very 'hands-on', were

Key for Speed's Map
1 St Michan's Church
2 St Mary's Abbey
3 The Innes of Court
4 Bridge Street
5 The Bridge
6 Newman's Tower
7 Fian's Castle
8 Wood Key
9 Merchants Key
10 The Hospital
11 St Augustine's
12 The College
13 Bridewell
14 Dame's Street
15 Dame's Gate
16 St Andrew's Church
17 St George's Lane
18 St Steven's Street
19 St Steven's Church
20 St Peter's Church
21 White Friars
22 St Michael le Pole Chr
23 The Castle
24 Fish Shambles
25 Wine Tavern St.
26 Woodstock Lane
27 Ram Lane
28 Cook Street
29 Ormond's Gate
30 Kaiser's Lane
31 St Audoen's Lane
32 St Michael's Lane
33 Christ Church Lane
34 St Audoen's Church
35 Christ Church
36 Schoolhouse Lane
37 St John's Church
38 Castle Street
39 Pole Gate
40 St Werburgh's Street
41 St Werburgh's Church
42 Skinners Row
43 St Nicholas Church
44 St Nicholas St
45 St Nicholas Gate
46 The Tholsel
47 St Michael's Church
48 High Street
49 Back Lane
50 New Gate
51 St Thomas Street
52 New Row
+ The Mills
53 Tennis Court Lane
54 Johns House
55 St James Street
56 St James Gate
57 St Catherine's Church
58 St Thomas Court
59 The Comb
60 New Street
61 St Francis Street
62 St Patrick's Street
63 St Patrick's Church
64 St Bride's Church
65 St Bride's Street
66 St Sepulchre's
67 St Kevin's Street
68 Cross Lane

Notes

Sheep St. (aka Ship St.), said to be no. 22, is to the right of the church.

No. 25, Wine Tavern St, is the next street to the left of Fish Shambles; the number is just below a towerhouse or gate in the middle of the street and is difficult to see.

No. 30 also needs to move to the street to the right.

The number '34' is on the area of the corn market.

The number on the street to the left of no. 44 is 49, not 40.

No. 54, Johns House, is an alms/hospital.

After Gilbert, v. 1, p. 10, the item at the west end of Castle St is the Pillory; there was also a water conduit, or public fountain on the Fishamble St side of this intersection, as noted on p. 56 of the same source, though Colm Lennon, in an email, puts this on the St Werburgh St side of this intersection. The shape of the item on the map looks more like the conduit than the pillory.

easily transmuted into Christianity. Figures of saints, holy wells, celebrations of the seasons, and the marking of birth and death were expressed in the symbols and materials used by people from time immemorial. Scholars were mostly concerned with the elaboration of biblical passages, the sorting out of Christ's divinity with regard to His humanity, and moral imperatives.

Then, in the sixteenth century, there were two interrelated turning-points: the Renaissance and the Reformation. Owing to an influx of Greek scholars after the conquest of Constantinople by people of Islamic faith in the fifteenth century, western European scholars rediscovered Greek philosophy. This was based more on a humanistic premise: man as the measure of all things rather than a biblically based monotheistic faith in God as the measure of all life. The technological advance of printing then facilitated the circulation of these ideas. This fostered a renaissance in intellectual life.

Another deeply distressing aspect of the Renaissance was the Copernican revolution, which demonstrated that the earth revolved around the sun. Copernicus's treatise was published in 1543. The replacement of the geocentric frame of reference with a heliocentric one further disoriented people's perspective. Not only were the basics of belief being questioned but also society's very understanding of humanity's place in the universe was being challenged. It was a lot to take in, and contributed quite profoundly to people's upset and distress. The Roman Catholic Church condemned Copernicus, while others saw his work as providing a release from a false understanding of the world.

All this intellectual turmoil contributed to an atmosphere in which the dominance of Rome could be challenged. Its corruption by unchecked power left it open to criticism and charges of betraying the original intent of Christianity. A German Augustinian monk, Martin Luther, publicly broke with Rome in 1517. It was an idea whose time had come; Christianity was being reformed.

This reformation, however, was based on an approach that critiqued developments of Christian theology and practices which had accrued over the centuries. Ordinary people, for whom faith was an experiential affair, generally were not as persuaded by a change in theological thinking. Those who held power through the Roman Church also opposed any change, whereas those who stood to gain by this challenge to Roman power, especially with regard to landownership, were more content to go along. These two seismic shifts in outlook and belief generated a tsunami of trauma across Europe, as violence became the medium through which change was enforced. Battle lines were drawn. Society's stable pillars were crumbling.

The Reformation was introduced into England and Ireland in the 1530s by Henry VIII, who had a lot to gain by declaring himself the head of the English Church. Initially, he apparently had not wished to instigate any significant theological or ritual changes. He simply wanted the top job in an otherwise unchanged institution. But as some English people came into contact with the Continental reformers, they pushed for these changes in England as well. In Ireland, however, the change that had the greatest impact in the sixteenth century was the dissolution of the monasteries. These centres of cultural and religious tradition had been present in Ireland since at least the sixth century. They held relics of saints, bodies of the deceased élites, and men and women who were revered as exemplars of the Christian life. In addition, they gave alms to the poor, ran hospitals for the sick, and taught schools that provided education for certain levels of society. Monasteries were very 'hands-on' places. (Even in England their closure provoked a revolt, known as the Pilgrimage of Grace.)

Living through the seventeenth century in Ireland was not easy. It was the most traumatic stretch of time to have been visited upon this island in the last 2,000 years. Despite a militarily peaceful four decades at the start, the gradually accelerating loss of landownership by the Gaelic inhabitants resulted in the collapse of their culture and society. Yet very few in Ireland today are aware of this story. One can read about it in any Irish history book that covers this century, but it will be a bird's-eye view, told from above, with little detail of what it looked and felt like for the people on the ground.

We are fortunate, then, to have the estate papers of a middle-ranking family whose story coincides with this century. These papers allow us to follow their rise and demise over this period. They interacted both with those in the highest levels of the government and with ordinary people of more humble station. We will see how their progenitor rode the rising tide of land acquisition and gained the status of a baronet, and then how the family was swallowed up in the continuing tumult at the end.

One lens through which to view this period, especially when doing so from the personal level, is that of trauma—the trauma of immense loss, of the constant threat of poverty and disenfranchisement, loss of the very words with which people thought and expressed themselves, and loss of how Gaelic people had, for time out of mind, celebrated and lived life year in and year out.

Trauma has both physiological and psychological effects. A traumatised body will either respond with action (fighting or fleeing) or it will collapse into lethargy and simply give up. Emotionally, this manifests as fear, panic and anger or as depression and resignation. Trauma's fear provokes a deep sense of insecurity, an anxiety that pervades a person's life. At a collective level, societal trauma also affects how a group makes meaning for themselves, how they understand their identity and role in the world.

People then search for some way to provide themselves with a sense of security, a feeling that they will be held safely, protected and allowed, even helped, to thrive. Traditionally, the two most common things to which people have looked for this kind of security have been religion and wealth/power. Religion, especially the monotheistic type, posits a dialogue with the deity so that people can understand what is expected by and from this deity. It is then hoped that compliance will prevent the onslaught of traumatic events. The option of power/wealth is more pragmatic. A group or individual gains power, often via control of resources, the military or money, and thereby protects themselves from external attack. If there are natural disasters, they are best placed to survive.

Recorded history generally consists of highly traumatic events—wars, famines, genocides, natural disasters or forced migrations. The writing of history has also included the interpretation of why such events happened. With the rise of Christianity, a belief in God's will was a central explanatory factor. For the Christian people of the seventeenth century, whether Catholic or Protestant, this focused on the punishment of sins committed and rewards for pleasing God. Without an awareness of the importance of this belief, it can be hard to make sense of some of the actions taken by the people of this period. For example, after the 1641 rebellion, in which Protestants in Ireland suffered significant loss, the explanation for this was that they had not been righteous enough and needed to be even more austere in their religious practice. In turn, this fuelled an increase in the number of radical Protestants.

This point of view regarding God's will was also held among the Gaelic intelligentsia. When reflecting on the demise of Gaelic power in the sixteenth and seventeenth centuries, they pointed to a failure to obey God's laws. The very parochial mind of the bardic poets did not hold the English responsible for the fall of Hugh O'Neill. Instead, 'If you had been submissive to God, who could have overthrown you?'[7]

Another element of the frame of reference was that the Christian God had people who were His chosen ones, favoured by Him and most likely to survive lethal catastrophes. With the Reformation, there was a push to know who was chosen, or 'of the elect'. One of the markers that was used to identify who was *not* of the elect was being a follower of the pope, said to be the antichrist, or a venerator of saints, which was characterised as idolatry. On the other hand, the Catholic Church held that it alone was the one true church, and that all others were heretics and damned to hell. With each side convinced that they alone were God's chosen ones, there was very little room for dialogue. Later, among Protestants, there was a further development which held that material prosperity/wealth was also an indication that one was among the elect.

Being 'elect' gave a person a sense of security and superiority. Those who did not believe that they were saved by Christ, or who refused to subscribe to this belief and stand with them, were thus considered inferior. They were not worthy of basic respect or what we would now call human rights. Such people were only useful as labourers for fuelling the profits of the chosen ones' estates. They were to be colonised by superior Europeans. The earth, too, was said to be at the service of the elect, there to be exploited for profit and progress.

It is impossible to understand fully the events of the seventeenth century without grasping this frame of reference with regard to how people saw life and one another. The notion of the equality of all people before the law and the deity, without qualification, is a much more recent idea, and not one subscribed to in that century.

The first chapter of this work will look at how Robert Kennedy got his start in his home city of Dublin, how his network evolved, who was in it, and what he did with those connections. He needed to build a secure base, to present a prosperous image to his fellow Dubliners, and to play the role of someone with money who was in the know and open for business. The second chapter looks at how, after this was adequately achieved, Robert used other ways to increase his affluence. With this he was able to expand into securing an estate for himself. Circumstances presented themselves that allowed him to gain a large amount of land in the nearby County Wicklow in the 1620s and 1630s.

The upheavals that characterise this century in Ireland are then explored in the third chapter. The onslaught of Thomas Wentworth, Earl of Strafford, head of the English government in Ireland from 1633 to 1641, taxed Kennedy's tenacity in retaining all that he had achieved. He nevertheless found new ways to expand his holdings and generate large amounts of money. The 1641 rebellion made thriving even more difficult, but once again he managed to hold tight through this period, and proved particularly adept at negotiating the transition from a royal government to the Cromwellian commonwealth. In Chapter 4 we see the family at their peak, with the granting of a baronetcy, offspring of the second generation marrying well, Court posts restored and a judgeship secured.

The twists and turns of the century finally managed to undo this upwardly mobile family, however, as several factors that we will examine in Chapter 5 brought them to an untimely end. In the final chapter, we will look at a very unexpected development, in which the last baronet converted to Catholicism and became a Benedictine.

It is relatively rare to have the estate papers of a family like the

Kennedys, newly minted Gaelic Protestants of the seventeenth century. Because there has been no previous detailing of their activities, finding out who they were has been an adventure in itself, revealing unexpected twists and turns. Their story illustrates the potential and the pitfalls of life in that century, tempting with the promise of riches but full of danger and ill luck.

1
Making it in 'the Cittie'

Our story begins with the origins of this Kennedy family—where they came from, how the first of the line, Robert, got his start, who helped him and what he did with that help. The factors that encouraged Gaelic families to migrate to Dublin in the early to mid-sixteenth century are not entirely clear. Some of them would have been cadet branches of leading septs who lost out in the competition for power, which had become more intense at this time.

To provide greater context, let us look at the political and cultural situation in Ireland since the Anglo-Norman invasion in the late twelfth century. The Anglo-Normans, despite their initial success in gaining power over much of the island, had by the fourteenth century been greatly reduced in their reach. Instead, they had married into the families of Gaelic lords and been drawn into the constant jockeying for dominance that characterised Gaelic society at that time.

The English Crown had made use of the head of the Anglo-Norman Fitzgerald family, Earls of Kildare, as their man on the ground and lord deputy or governor of Ireland. It saved the Crown a lot of money, as the earls were responsible for maintaining their own political power. They did so by using traditional Gaelic structures and participating fully in Gaelic culture, with its brehon law, bards, ollamhs, physicians and other Gaelic orders.

The Fitzgerald who became the earl in 1514 found himself in conflict with the Butlers of Kilkenny as well as being disliked by Pale officials because of his Gaelic ways. Henry VIII, who had become king in 1509, took this as an opportunity to sack Fitzgerald and replace him with an Englishman, Thomas Howard, Earl of Surrey (and Anne Boleyn's uncle). Howard only lasted a year, however, before the practicality of having a local earl reasserted itself. It was the Butlers, Earls of Ormond, who then received the nod. This, of course, rankled with the Fitzgeralds, who continued the country-wide penchant for fighting with their neighbours. In 1533 another Englishman was put in as the lord deputy. In the meantime, the next Earl of Kildare, 'Silken Thomas', had led a rebellion, which failed owing to a lack of support from his fellow Gaelic leaders. Thomas and his uncles were executed despite a promise of pardon. Their ill treatment provoked an uproar throughout Ireland. Henry then confiscated Fitzgerald's lands.

To further complicate the situation, Henry broke with Rome in 1534, making him militarily vulnerable to France and Spain and alienating the Catholic Church. Gaelic leaders rallied against the English in armed revolt, this time supporting the new Earl of Kildare. English forces repelled them but they were not entirely subdued, leaving the island in a state of severe tension. The English governor at the time, Lord Grey, was recalled and executed for treason on account of his inability to handle the situation to Henry's satisfaction. Fierce fighting continued for the next few years. In 1540 Sir Anthony St Leger was appointed lord deputy. He proceeded to inflict such massive damage on the Irish that many of the élite were broken and starving.

At this point St Leger, with Henry's agreement, offered the option of what would later be called 'surrender and regrant'. In exchange for adopting English ways and language, any Gaelic lord who submitted to the king in person, and surrendered his title to his lands, would be made an earl and have a seat in the Irish parliament. These lords would hold their lands at the pleasure of the king and pay him rent. (This last requirement was what had persuaded Henry to accept this deal.) They would also adopt primogeniture, meaning that their eldest son would be guaranteed to succeed them as earl. In their very weakened state, the promise of a title and the exaltation of their family, not part of the traditional Gaelic approach, won over many of the Gaelic leaders. Though apparently not seen as a significant departure from tradition at the time, these changes to Gaelic practices gave the English a 'foot in the door' of Gaelic society which was to prove its undoing in the end. Prominent sons were sent to England for their education, becoming Protestant and following English law.

With the enactment of primogeniture, cadet branches of leading families no longer had much hope of becoming chief of their nation. This may be the reason why some of them looked for other options for advancement. The city of Dublin was an obvious destination. The activities of trading were attractive to those who had been dislodged from their ancestral lands. These ambitious men were able to do very

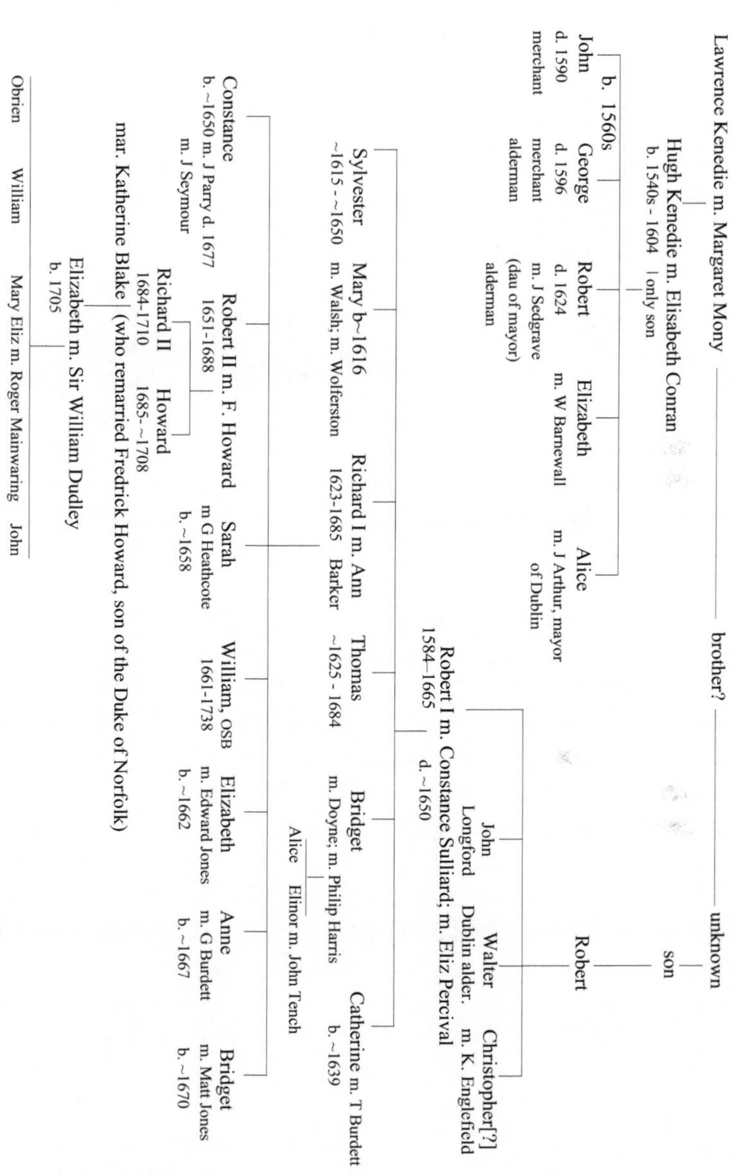

Illus. 3—Kennedy family tree.

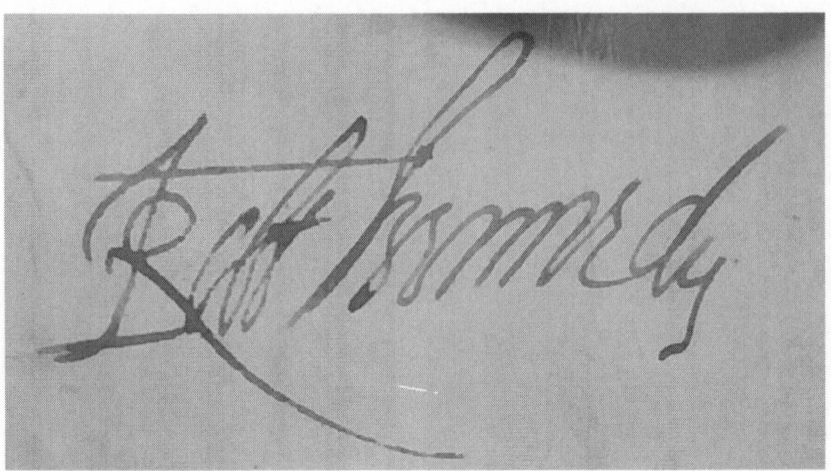

Robert Kennedy's signature.

well financially as merchants, acting as middlemen in the transfer of goods, and able to travel abroad and deal with foreigners. Despite noticeable hostility to people of Gaelic background within Dublin, they gradually rose to prominence, becoming thoroughly Anglicised in the process.

One man, Lawrence O'Kenedie, who was most probably from County Tipperary (though Wicklow and Meath have also been suggested[1]), had opted to move to Dublin. Although it is not documented, it is quite possible that at least one of his brothers came with him. A later direct descendant of Lawrence commissioned his genealogy from the Ulster King of Arms in 1607.[2] Having one's genealogy recorded and being given permission to use a coat of arms were ways of marking that a family had achieved significant status and wealth. From his genealogy we can also see that the Mount Kennedy branch did not stem directly from Lawrence but may well have descended from one of his brothers (see Illus. 3).

Apart from his name, Robert, nothing is known about the father of the immediate progenitor of the Mount Kennedy baronets,[3] nor about where the family was living within the walls of Dublin. An examination of Dublin's Church of Ireland parish registers, however, along with comments by Gilbert as to which parishes contained more 'papists', would suggest St John's parish as a likely candidate. Its registers are the oldest that have been preserved, going back to 1619, and, very fortunately, they have been published, with an index. This reveals that there were a large number of Kennedys living in this parish, along with a large number of papists, according to Gilbert. The Kennedys listed would have been Protestants, of course, which also lets us know that this group had split—some remaining staunch Catholics while others had accommodated themselves to the times.

In addition, St John's parish would have extended to the quays and would have been a location favoured by merchants, giving convenient access to incoming goods. Friends and acquaintances of Robert Kennedy also lived in this parish, such as Sir Francis Annesley, a Charles Smith (the later brother-in-law?), and families of Carrolls and Conrans. An Alderman Kennedy (see further below) was also said to have owned property on Fishamble Street, which was in this parish.

The first baronet's initial appearance in any historical record is found in the *Calendar of State Papers of Ireland*, where in 1602 Robert Kennedy is described as the second chamberlain of the Court of the Exchequer, one of the Four Courts of Ireland.[4] If it is assumed that he was eighteen years old at that time, this would give him a birth year of 1584. The very fact that he became a clerk in the court system means that he would have been literate in English. His education, most probably in a Catholic school run by members of a religious order, would have been through Latin, with possible instruction in the European languages in which these men would have been educated. Generally, only families with a middle-class income would have been able to afford such schooling for their sons, and perhaps daughters. From this we can further deduce that his father may have been a merchant or a clerk.

Growing up in Dublin in the 1590s was less than optimal, however.[5] Like much of the rest of Europe, the people of Dublin were suffering the hardships of famine, plague and war. This Irish famine was specifically the consequence of harvest failures for three years in a row, in 1594–6, which had exhausted the usual reserves set aside for a summer of bad weather. People were dying not only of starvation but also of plague, owing to the weakened condition engendered by hunger. Indeed, the city's population had never fully recovered from the Black Death in the mid-fourteenth century. The wars across Europe often played out the tensions set in motion by the Reformation. People battled for the triumph of their beliefs, or at least for the right to hold them.

In Ulster in 1593, Hugh O'Neill, then Earl of Tyrone, had commenced a war against the encroaching English government. Initially, he had notable successes against English troops. Then the English adopted a 'scorched earth' policy, destroying all sources of food in a locale, thus weakening the ability of the Irish to fight back. This further increased the scarcity of food, and especially the price of grain. In addition, Dublin was particularly vulnerable to attack owing to a long-standing lack of maintenance of the city walls.

There was great consternation among Dubliners as regards their safety; attacks were anticipated and a night guard set. They were very glad to see the arrival of English troops but, to add insult to injury, those troops were then billeted in their houses and had to be fed. In a time of scarce and expensive food, with Dubliners dying for lack of it, they had to feed soldiers as well. Nevertheless, as bad as life was up to this point in the 1590s, it was about to become devastatingly worse.

As the war progressed, royal authorities had to import armaments, including gunpowder, to fight against O'Neill. Because of sand bars in the harbour, all goods coming in had to be loaded onto smaller boats, known as 'lighters', and then brought to the quayside. Such a shipment of powder was being unloaded on 11 March 1597. Against all procedural rules, it had been piled together rather than being immediately moved to Dublin Castle as each keg was landed. Suddenly, just at 1 p.m., 140 barrels exploded. The death and devastation were immense: 126 people were killed, the equivalent of 10,000 people in the present-day city. Buildings along the waterfront were blown away, and very few structures in the walled environs escaped some form of damage. It would take decades for the city to recover.

Growing up in such an environment would have had a profound effect on the children of the city. Robert, aged about thirteen in 1597, was the eldest son in this Kennedy family. He had brothers, John and Walter, both of whom appear in the Mount Kennedy estate papers. In Illus. 3 there is a question mark next to Christopher's name. He was the husband of Kathryn Englefield, and Walter, in his 1672 will, named her brother Henry as a 'brother[-in-law]'. It would seem more likely that he is one of the sons of Robert the alderman, as no other mention of him has been found, except for these sons taken in wardship. (As so often happened, the presence of female siblings is unattested, they disappearing into the families of their husbands.) The three boys, despite their relative privilege, would have felt the impact of death, sickness and the intense fear of those living in a war zone. How many of their relatives died in this decade? If they were living in St John's parish, it is possible that their house was damaged and that they or their parents were injured in the 1597 explosion.

Because human beings are so complex, individuals confronted with nearly the same level of trauma can have very different reactions, within certain parameters. Whichever way they responded, however, such impacts would have had lifelong repercussions. Robert's father had the worry of keeping his family safe and fed. There is never a mention of his mother, and perhaps she perished in this decade. The younger boys were helpless bystanders. How would these years affect their functioning as adults?

The other pertinent aspect of Robert Kennedy's profile that can be inferred is that at some point in his clerk's career he had taken the Oath of Supremacy, acknowledging the king as the head of the English (and Irish) Church, and had become a Protestant. Under Elizabeth I, Catholics had been allowed to participate in the government of Ireland and the city of Dublin. This was rapidly changing, however, and it is quite likely that, being an astute young man, Robert could see that the way forward would be to join the ranks of those who saw the Church of Rome as a betrayer of Christianity. Later documents confirm that he was a Protestant but that his brothers were Catholics.[6]

Religious affiliation, particularly since the Reformation, had become a contentious aspect of one's social identity. Here we see an educated young man making a choice that many others of his heritage would regard as a betrayal of that identity. We don't know exactly when Robert took the Oath. Elizabeth did not die until 24 March 1603, so Robert may have been able initially to secure his post without it.

Hugh O'Neill was finally defeated in 1603. He capitulated just at the time when Elizabeth died, though he was not told of her death until afterwards. He was so crushed at this point that he had grovelled at the feet of the English leader, pleading for mercy and promising allegiance if he were spared. His ignominious surrender would demonstrate the fate of anyone who dared to rebel against English might. Although an Ulsterman, he had been hosted by a Catholic Anglo-Irish family, the Hovendans of Balgriffin in north County Dublin, after he became a ward of the State, and was every inch an English gentleman. His occasional presence on Dublin's streets in his earlier years would have attracted the attention of many of the young men of Gaelic background, who would have seen him as an example of Gaelic success within an Anglicised Ireland. Though O'Neill was restored to power in his Ulster area, his downfall was a warning to others who risked the obstinacy of maintaining Gaelic ways. Only four years later O'Neill and his supporters among the Ulster élite fled Ireland, in the vain hope of returning to fight another day.

The sudden and unexpected departure of O'Neill and others is known as the Flight of the Earls. This is a typical trauma response, which can occur at any time after the event. It occasioned the collapse of Gaelic culture in the north. Bernadette Cunningham has pointed out that Gaelic society depended on the chief for its traditional functioning. His kinsmen would provide him with his yearly income from the produce of the land. This, in turn, was used to support the bardic poets, physicians, ollamhs, language experts and others, as well as to provide generous hospitality to all comers. With the loss of the chief, the poets were the ones to articulate their sudden loss of employment and collapse of identity. They observed that it would have been better if they had been tradesmen who could earn a living from the use of their hands. Some emigrated to the Continent, where they found employment suitable to their literate skills.[7]

When James I ascended the throne, tolerance for Catholics in State and city posts diminished rapidly. He tackled Dublin's aldermen, most of whom were Catholics, head on. The aldermen were a group of 24 leading citizens of Dublin, mostly merchants, who ran the city. Confronted with the demand that the mayor take the Oath of Supremacy, William Gough in 1603 declined to serve in this office. He was then threatened with a £2,000 fine for his avoidance of the office. Seven of the aldermen protested by absenting themselves and were imprisoned.

The following year, the mayoral candidate again refused to take office. He was fined £300 and stripped of his liberty of the city, losing the right to conduct business there. He was also imprisoned for two years. In 1605 he was joined by a number of his fellow aldermen,[8] among whom was Robert Kennedy, merchant, who was probably our Robert's second cousin once removed and one of the wealthiest men in the city at the time. With such intense pressure, it is likely that our second chamberlain had embraced the Protestant faith at the latest by 1605, when the Oath of Supremacy was made mandatory for mayors.[9]

What is it that pushes a person to forsake their social and cultural identity? One answer to this question is collective trauma. When a people is sorely oppressed and stripped of its cultural institutions, the impact is manifested at a collective level. This is a

> 'blow to the basic tissues of social life that damages the bonds attaching people together and impairs the prevailing sense of communality. The collective trauma works its way slowly and even

> insidiously into the awareness of those who suffer from it, so it [is] a gradual realization that the community no longer exists as an effective source of support and that an important part of [one's identity] has disappeared.'[10]

By the early 1600s, those who had witnessed the defeat of the Earl of Tyrone, and his later flight, knew at a gut level that to be Gaelic was to be part of a fading and unsustainable way of life. Being a Catholic was a feature associated with a person who held to Gaelic ways.

Was Robert a betrayer, or a pragmatist, or a person enlightened by a conversion experience? When such a personal choice has profound social and economic consequences, is it really possible to decide which of these labels is the most accurate? Becoming a Protestant was a smart move on Robert's part. In his heart of hearts, did he believe any of it? Where did he see himself in terms of the God of Abraham, Isaac and Jacob?

Nevertheless, despite the ominous signs, there were many Catholics who resisted any change in their religious affiliation, opting to fight rather than collapse. Indeed, Robert's older cousin, who likewise sidestepped the office of mayor when it was his turn to take it on, was imprisoned twice for refusing to betray his religion. None of his seven sons produced an heir, and his family faded into obscurity. In contrast, Alderman Thomas Carroll's son, James, took the Oath with his father's approval. This allowed Thomas to let James serve as mayor in his stead and saved the family's fortunes. Indeed, he was made mayor an unprecedented four times, greatly enhancing their coffers.

It is in the younger Robert Kennedy's generation that we can see the effects of the trauma inflicted in the previous century and the longer-term impact of surrender and regrant. As described above, he had also suffered the trauma of the quayside explosion, and the impact of the Nine Years War on Dubliners. His personal survival had been seriously threatened. His response was one of intense ambition, full of fight and schemes.

Whether Catholic or Protestant, how did Robert initially get that all-important first job—the post at the Exchequer? To answer this question, we must look ahead to the people who appear in the sources as part of Robert's network. The earliest of these is Sir James Carroll (d. 1639), who belonged to a family of merchants originally from the Tipperary/Offaly area. He, like his father, had become a Dublin alderman, and was appointed chief chamberlain of the Exchequer in 1597. In 1600 he was the deputy treasurer at war.[11] It is quite likely that he still had some influence at the Exchequer (though he had surrendered his patent) and would have been well placed to provide a post for Robert. In later years there would be an exchange of letters between Robert and James, wherein Carroll spoke very warmly to him and signed himself 'your loving cousin'.[12]

Robert, of course, had another important link with James—they had both converted to Protestantism. James's adherence to the Established Church was evidently a matter of convenience rather than conviction, as he was known to be a harbourer of priests. Robert's degree of conviction is less clear. Reflecting on his later choices of association, one might think him possibly aligned with radical Protestants. Yet, given his flexibility after their fall from power, it may be more likely that he was simply pragmatic—he did whatever furthered his career and power.

Having been an aspiring young man, Robert's main goal appears to have been to make his fortune in a rapidly changing Ireland. He would have been aware that there had lately been an influx of English Protestants, of varying persuasions, some of whom had been doing very well for themselves. A relatively high percentage of these were radical Protestants, sometimes known as Puritans.

After Henry VIII's initial break with Rome, Queen Mary had attempted to make Catholicism the official religion again. During her reign, some of the English Protestants fled to the Continent, where they encountered the more radical Protestantism of Calvin and others. When Mary's successor, Elizabeth I, then swung back to Protestantism, these radicalised Protestants returned to England. Since, however, Elizabeth was trying to maintain a balance between many who wanted to remain Catholic and the Crown's favouring of Anglicanism, these more radical reformers were not warmly received. After frustration in England, some of the more radical Protestants moved on to English colonies, such as Ireland and later again to Massachusetts, where they had freer rein to practise their forms of Protestantism.[13]

One of the newly arrived Protestants in the late sixteenth century was Richard Boyle, who was based in Cork. He had been employed as an official in the English government of Ireland specifically to use a legal stratagem to take land from unsuspecting landowners on the grounds of insufficient title. He had used his position corruptly to gain vast amounts of Irish land for himself, particularly in Munster.

In general terms, the process by which Boyle had managed to cheat the English Crown out of titles to lands in Ireland in the 1590s involved several government officers—an escheator (someone who determined the validity of a land title or whether it had been sold legally), a deputy surveyor-general, one of numerous clerks in the Exchequer system, a clerk under the auditor-general, also in the Exchequer, and a seneschal (sheriff). Boyle himself was the deputy escheator (unsupervised by the ailing escheator) from 1590 to 1596, with Francis Capstock as the deputy surveyor-general; the other Exchequer clerk is unnamed.[14] The sheriff in Kerry was Boyle's stepfather-in-law.[15] Boyle's network continued to expand despite some setbacks.

With the co-operation of these officers, Boyle identified the 'concealed' or forfeited titles, undervalued them, and then purposefully failed to register them properly with the other government offices and courts. In his own time, he then purchased these lands at the discounted prices that he himself had reckoned. It is quite likely that the surveyor-general at the time, Sir Geoffrey Fenton, was aware of what was going on. He would have turned a blind eye, as he was also an ambitious Protestant; his daughter Katherine went on to become Boyle's second wife in 1603. A greedy government can sometimes be outfoxed by an even greedier junior government official.

After his start, facilitated by James Carroll, the centre of Robert Kennedy's primary networking circle developed around William Parsons (Illus. 4). The latter would have been an obvious person of interest for Robert, who evidently was looking for help to do something similar to what Boyle had done. Parsons (1570?–1650) had arrived in Ireland from Leicestershire sometime in the 1590s after embracing radical Protestantism as a youth. He initially assisted his uncle, Sir Geoffrey Fenton, and took up the office of surveyor-general when his uncle passed it on to him in 1602.[16] In a country where gaining land was a priority, this was a coveted post. It was also a part of the Court of the Exchequer, whose judicial branch was only one of a number of bodies therein. To make a clandestine land-grabbing operation work, however, Parsons would also need contacts among the chamberlains, who kept track of land transactions and their values. An ambitious young man like Robert Kennedy would have suited his purposes admirably.

William Parsons was related to Richard Boyle via his cousin Katherine Fenton, who was Boyle's second wife. Parsons subsequently used his own ample supply of children to craft a very powerful network. His eldest son married Lettice Loftus, eldest daughter of Sir Adam Loftus of Rathfarnham. Catherine, the eldest of his seven daughters,

Illus. 4—Portrait of Sir William Parsons.

married Sir James Barry, first Baron Barry of Santry. The second, Margaret, married Thomas Stockdale of Bilton Park, Yorkshire; the third, Elizabeth, married Sir William Ussher of Grange Castle, Co. Wicklow (grandson of Sir William Ussher, clerk of the Council); the fourth, Jane, married Sir John Hoey, Knight, of Dunganstown, Co. Wicklow; the fifth, Mary, married Arthur Hill of Hillsborough, Co. Down; and the sixth, Anne, married Sir Paul Davis, Secretary of State (Ireland). Lastly, Judith married Thomas Whyte of Redhills, Co. Cavan.[17] The scope and diversity of Parsons's reach were impressive, and he used it to his greatest advantage.

Parsons's quest for land was intense, and he was zealous in promoting plantations throughout much of Ireland. When some at court in London challenged this policy, Parsons was quick to offer them a cut of the profits, and opposition immediately changed to enthusiastic support. In keeping with his tendency to radical Protestantism, Parsons was also keen to make sure that Catholics, whether English or Irish, did not participate in landownership in Ireland. The breadth of his duplicity, his manipulation of factions and other reprehensible activities are beyond the scope of this work. Some scholars suggest that his thwarting of the king's intention to deal fairly with the Irish Confederation in the early 1640s was an important factor in driving a wedge between Protestant and Catholic landowners, and in the wholesale dispossession of Irish Catholics.[18] The fact that Robert Kennedy was a close ally of Parsons tells us a lot about the younger man.

Two other associates of Robert's were William Rowlls and John Pue. Rowlls was a subseneschal (assistant sheriff), an MP for Newcastle, Co. Dublin, in the 1613–15 parliament (along with Parsons) and later a commissioner for the plantation of the Byrnes' country (north-east Wicklow), again with Parsons.[19] He appears along with Robert in documents concerning King's Letters land grants, of which more later.

John Pue, alias ap Hugh, a Welshman, was a clerk, later a Dublin sheriff[20] and finally the registrar of His Majesty's High Commission Court of Ireland.[21] He was one of the many 'New English' men who arrived in Ireland in this period to make their fortunes. He would later live in a house on St Nicholas Street (owned by Robert Kennedy), own a tower-house in County Wicklow about seven miles south of Robert's, and be a member of the trust that Robert set up to facilitate his land purchases in Wicklow. Interestingly, the Kennedys would have quite a lot of interaction with Welshmen in the coming years.

Other members of this trust were William Parsons, his eldest son Richard, Sir William Bishop, alderman and mayor of the Dublin Staple, Richard Barry, alderman (a father-in-law of Parsons's daughter Catherine) and also part of the staple, Nicholas Kelly, alderman, Thomas Stockdale, a son-in-law of Parsons and the clerk of the pells and tallies (an office in Exchequer), and Bernard Grasswell, a yeoman in Kishoge, Co. Dublin.[22] Thomas Stockdale was someone whose government office gave him access to a lot of money; he was also a business friend of Robert's, through whom he had bought an interest in a house on St Nicholas Street. The fact that three aldermen were among Robert's trustees tells us how high his networking had reached within Dublin's élite.

The Dublin Staple, originally set up to regulate the export trade of staple goods, was later used to record and keep track of money lent and borrowed by a wide variety of individuals. Access to money via people involved in the Staple, or otherwise through their government office, could have been useful in Robert's land activities. He would have known all these men well enough to trust them with his high-value personal property.

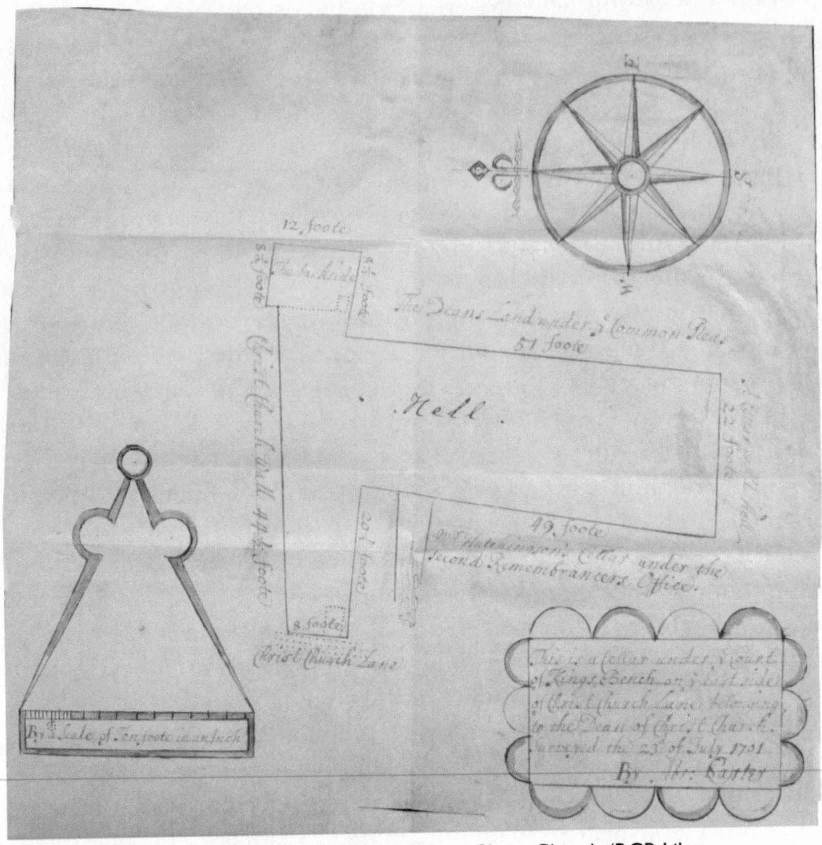

Illus. 5—Small map of second chamberlain's office in Christ Church (RCB Library, C6/3/6/2/2[15228]; used with permission).

Robert's clerical post would have been in the auditor-general's office within the Court of the Exchequer. Initially, in 1602, he would have sat in Dublin Castle, but the area occupied by the Courts was in a building that had become very dilapidated. Worse yet, it was immediately over the cellar in which the gunpowder was stored. With the explosion of 1597 still fresh in people's memories, it was decided to move the Courts to the buildings that had been the Dominican priory, located on the north side of the river. There was a plan to erect a new building for the Courts, but then it was noticed that there were rooms in the Christ Church complex which could be repurposed at much less cost. This was done, and the Four Courts took up residence there in 1608 (Illus. 5 and 21). They would remain there until 1796, when the long-planned new building was erected on the north quay.[23]

Robert's main work was to keep the books for moneys received by the Exchequer from those who owed rent to the Crown.[24] In terms of income, it provided him with his basic salary and the permission to charge the public for making handwritten copies of whatever documentation they required of his office and other paperwork.[25] Probably the most lucrative aspect of his post, however, was the option to do favours for land speculators—and the associated bribes.

It would appear that by 1607 Robert had accumulated enough money to enter the housing market in Dublin. Once again, his 'loving cousin' facilitated this next step, when James Carroll sold him an interest in a house on St Nicholas Street for £10.[26] It is also possible that James lent him the money for this. James apparently had a lot of money. Whether he had made this as a merchant or had been helping out in the land scams is probably unknowable, but certainly he lent money in significant amounts. He was appointed chief remembrancer of the Exchequer by Lord Deputy Chichester in June 1609, and was also knighted in that year. In the same month, he lent Richard Colman £1,000 so that he could gain the office of the joint chief remembrancer[27] along with James himself.

Robert Kennedy's first documented interaction with William Parsons came in October 1609, when we see that Robert had witnessed a lease agreement between Parsons and Patrick Browne, alderman, for the Browne estate of 140 acres and a mansion in Kishoge, south-west Co. Dublin. This document also testifies to the gradual decline of the Catholic Anglo-Norman Browne family, who were losing out at this time owing to their religion. Parsons was renting the estate for 81 years after providing £150 upfront and an annual rent of £20.[28] Robert Kennedy would later own this estate.

Robert continued to benefit from his connection with James Carroll when in May 1612 he was appointed joint chief chamberlain,[29] which would have helped his income. It evidently also made marriage possible. In 1614, at about 30 years of age, he married Constance Sulliard, said to be English-born,[30] the first daughter of Jonas Sulliard of Dublin and Margaret, daughter of Ralph Sankey of Fassaroe, Co. Dublin. Their first son, Sylvester, was born in 1615.[31]

Robert's motives for marrying Constance appear to have been very much concerned with increasing his network and local land acquisition. Her grandfather on her mother's side, Ralph Sankey, first appears in Dublin records as a Dublin alderman and a sheriff for the city. In 1592, he was one of six men charged with collecting money to finish building the new university (Trinity). Two years later he was the sheriff for Fassaroe, which at that time, prior to the shiring of County Wicklow in 1606, was in County Dublin.[32] This would have put him in touch with Pierce/Peter Talbot, whose family had held the manors of Rathdown and Fassaroe since 1537.[33] Ralph's daughter, Alice, became the second wife of this Talbot, while his other daughter,[34] Margaret, married Jonas Sulliard.

There is a record of Sir John Sulliard (1518–1575) who was a prominent East Anglian magistrate, landowner, High Sheriff, knight, a Justice of the Court of King's Bench, and standard-bearer, but also strongly Roman Catholic in his religious affiliation. He had been very instrumental in securing the throne for Queen Mary, and sat in parliament during her reign.[34a] Jonas Sulliard would probably have been his grandson, given that his daughter used the coat of arms of these Sulliards. It may be that Sankey's daughter Margaret went to England and married Jonas there. Eventually, she moved back to Ireland with Jonas.

Later, their son Thomas married Pierce's daughter, Katherine Talbot, a daughter of his first wife (so there was no blood relationship).[35] Katherine's eldest brother was Bernard — more of him later. When Robert married into the Sulliards in the mid-1610s, he evidently became a trustee for Peter Talbot as part of his new network.

Later, Ralph Sankey is also said to be an apothecary. He was obviously a man of some standing. There is no further record of him thereafter, apart from his death in 1619.[36] George Sankey, a dyer in Dublin, appears to have been Ralph's brother.[37] He owned property on St Nicholas Street, including an interest in Jenefields Inns. George and his wife had no children.

This 'Inns' was actually an ancient tower-house and hall built by Geoffrey de Geneville ('Jenefields' being a corruption of this Anglo-Norman name) in the thirteenth century. The building itself, part of the city walls, was feeling its age in the early seventeenth century, but it also had a large garden and orchard that backed on to the houses on the east side of St Nicholas Street. It was this land which may well have attracted Robert to make a connection with the Sankeys of Dublin. (There was another large group of Sankeys in the midlands, but there is apparently no documented connection between them.) He knew, perhaps owing to his Exchequer work, of the linkage between his wife's family's property and this large site.

Like Robert, the Sulliards evidently were an up-and-coming family. Sankey Sulliard, the eldest son of Jonas,[38] was also an apothecary and a merchant. Around the same year that Constance married Robert, he was admitted to the Dublin franchise as an apprentice, and rose through the ranks to become the mayor in 1650. This date would mark them as a radical Protestant family, since the Cromwellians were then in control in Ireland.[39] Even more importantly, Jonas and Margaret had two other sons and three other daughters. It is impossible to ascertain when Constance's siblings would have married, though the daughters at least were probably married after Constance, as she was the eldest. A later list of their marriage partners reveals another significant network in Robert's life.

Also in 1615, Robert began collecting properties in County Dublin for himself. After a complicated series of legal transactions, he came to hold an interest in the townland of Balgaddy (south-east of Lucan and east of Adamstown), contiguous with Kishoge to its west.[40] The family would continue to own these lands until the end of the century.

All this activity, and especially his connection to William Parsons, had brought Robert Kennedy to the notice of other land speculators. In 1616 an exchange of letters between Robert and Theobald Burke, later Baron of Brittas, Co. Limerick, was begun. Theobald was seeking advice on his land speculation in Queen's County (Laois). He was quite obsequious in his language, and later requested Robert's intercession with Parsons and others. Judging by the content of later letters, it would seem that Brittas was at least let down by Robert, if not outright betrayed by him, to the latter's gain. (By 1639 he had taken a case against Robert for not honouring a contract of work in full.)[41] This consultation was carried on at a distance, but it is quite possible that others located in Dublin, or near enough to come personally, may also have consulted Robert about this area of his expertise.

To give some indication of how hard-nosed Robert Kennedy was, there is a September 1616 record of his having taken a case against his colleague in the chief chamberlain's office, complaining that the other man, Nicholas Heward, was paid more than himself even though they were doing the same work. To settle the dispute, Robert requested that William Parsons and James Carroll be mediators. Needless to say, he won his case.[42] Then in January 1616/17 he gained a small income (£4) from an annuity in Jenefields Inns, purchasing it for £8.[43]

Nine months later, Robert paid £40 for a house 'lately built' on the east side of St Nicholas Street. Thomas Stockdale, one of Parsons's sons-

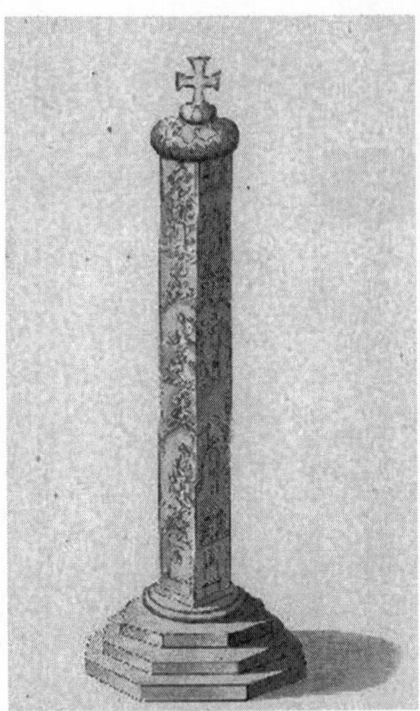

Illus. 6—The 20ft high Market Cross, High Street, Dublin. (https://upload.wikimedia.org/wikipedia/commons/8/8b/The_Market_Cross%2C_Dublin.jpg)

in-law as well as the clerk of pells in the Exchequer system, held it as a trustee for Robert's sole use. George Sankey was a witness to the transaction[44] and was actually one of his neighbours on the street. This purchase would have marked Robert's upward movement in Dublin and it became his residence. St Nicholas Street ran between a southern gate of the city and the Market Cross on the High Street, a distance of less than 500ft. High Street was the most prestigious

Illus. 7—The Tholsel, Dublin. (Source Unknown)

Illus. 8—Façade of the church of St Nicholas Within the Walls, Dublin. (Source Unknown)

residential street at the time. James Carroll, Thomas Bishop and William Parsons lived on the High Street, just around the corner (go up to the Market Cross and turn left) from Robert's house[45] (Illus. 6). The Tholsel, a multi-purpose town hall, was on the south-east corner of this intersection, just north of the medieval church of St Nicholas Within the Walls[46] (Illus. 7 and 8). When Robert was going to work, he had but to continue on past the Market Cross and go a short distance down Christ Church Lane (what is now the upper part of Winetavern Street). The entrance to the Four Courts complex was on the right.

Dublin's housing stock in the first two decades of this century was not impressive. Many of the dwellings were single-storey thatched cottages of mud and wattle walls, built in the preceding centuries. The buildings of larger construction would still bear the damage of the 1597 explosion. Only a few years later, there are receipts in Robert's records detailing the purchase of a large amount of timber for building. It seems fairly clear that he began to develop the houses on his side of

Illus. 9—A cagework house. (Source Unknown)

the street. Indeed, it is possible that he had built the house in which he was living. The most popular style of house at that time is one known as 'open cagework' (Illus. 9), generally of at least two storeys and sometimes expanding outward on the upper floors.

Not content with his post of chief chamberlain in the auditor-general's office, in February 1617/18 Robert also gained the post of clerk in the Court of Faculties,[47] located in the Court of the Chancery.[48] This was a post that had been instituted after the break with Rome to deal with all ecclesiastical matters that previously would have been sent to Rome. It included such things as the appointment of notaries public, verifying the value of various bishoprics in Ireland and enquiring into titles to hold benefices.[49] Robert would retain this post for the next ten years.[50] It would have increased his network considerably, putting him in contact with the clergy of the Established Church, not to mention church property. Interestingly, John Pue took over this post in 1628, after Robert surrendered it, and held it until he died in March 1660/1.[51]

Robert was obviously becoming a person to be taken account of in the real estate business. To mark his increasing status, he was granted his coat of arms by the Ulster King of Arms at this time. According to Daniel Molyneux, arms 'were the chiefest and most usuall invention of many other things devised by antiquitie for comendinge to posteritie the worth and good desertes of men of note and qualitie that thereby the memorie of theire well doinge might be derived beyond the narrowe boundes of this short and transitory life'.[52] (See his coat of arms on the frontispiece.)

The figure of three knights' helmets is the standard one for all Irish Kennedys (but differs from Kennedys in Scotland). The central image is the distinguishing feature for different branches of these families. It is not clear why Robert was given a scallop shell in the centre, as it is usually associated with those who have made a long pilgrimage. (It would suggest that perhaps one of his ancestors had done just this.) In one of the Funeral Entries, however, his arms have a small, open, upright hand in a shield in the middle.[53] This 'red hand of Ulster' is the mark of a baronet. John Kennedy's arms have a shield with four quadrants. Two, diagonally set, have the three knights' helmets, with the other two quadrants containing a similar figure but with three merchant ships, thus incorporating the arms of his wife's family.[54] In other images, his arms have the traditional three helmets with three small ships in the centre.[55] In a funeral entry for Walter Kennedy, a scallop shell is used in the centre.[56] Alderman Kennedy's arms have a five-pointed star in this place.

Robert's pay was increasing, and his perquisites and contributions on the side would have bolstered his finances. He was sought after as a consultant for land-dealing, and was well connected with William Parsons and Sir James Carroll and their circles of influence. Indeed, in November 1618 Parsons involved him in a land transaction in County Wicklow in which the older man rented portions of Kilmurry townland, parish of Newcastle, to Matthew O'Cullen.[57] Both Robert and his brother Walter, a merchant, were witnesses to this event. In 1619 a king's grant of over £10 to Walter Coppinger included Robert Kennedy's four houses on St Nicholas Street, said to have been lately built.[58] Robert would have had little difficulty in regaining possession, which involved paying the fees to do so.

Meanwhile, on the more mundane side of life, Robert was running up a debt at Alderman Kennedy's shop (these Kennedys were probably his wealthy relatives). In addition to timber, he had bought fancy cloth and fixings to look the part of a successful man about town. Extant listings of the cloth and decorations mention some very elegant fabrics, such as taffeta, silk, camlet, broad gold lace, fine black felt, ribbons, silk points and figurettes (perhaps some sort of jewellery), in colours of gold, blue, scarlet and black, of French and Flemish manufacture. There is also mention of suits for him and gowns for his wife.[59] One of his tailors is said to be Thomas Carroll. James's father, Thomas, is said to have been a tailor as well, so perhaps this was a cousin of James's.[60] Most intriguing in these bits of paper is the phrase 'your father's man'. This is the only reference to Robert's father anywhere in the extant estate papers.

Robert was evidently living beyond his means and had been borrowing money from James Carroll. In July 1620 James forgave him all the money he owed,[61] but the release does not specify the amount involved. Despite his financial difficulties, Robert continued to demonstrate the drive and financial risk-taking characteristic of the upwardly mobile.

His ambitions were rewarded five years later in 1625, when James Carroll resigned as the chief remembrancer of the Exchequer on 30 September and Robert took over the post the next day. He had to take out a £950 loan from Carroll to buy the pre-emption of the post[62]—this after James had signed himself 'your loving friend' in an August note.[63] Robert's brother, John, had become the other chief remembrancer six months earlier, after Sir Dudley Norton had resigned his position.[64]

John Kennedy was closely aligned with Robert. Although Robert is said to have been the second chamberlain in 1602, his patent was not issued until January 1610/11. When he became chief chamberlain in May 1612 (having bought the reversion), it was a further year before John became the second chamberlain in July 1613. It would seem plausible that Robert had at least helped this to happen. It is therefore curious that John, still only the second chamberlain, became the joint chief remembrancer in 1625, six months prior to Robert's achieving this post. By that time the brothers had also engaged in some land purchases in County Longford in the early 1620s. John had married Margaret, the only child of Major William Meares. The Major had a house on Skinners Row (the narrow lane between High Street and Castle Street, entered by taking a right at the Market Cross). She gave John 22 children, though only nine of these survived her death in 1648. By 1654 he had married another English woman, Mary Goare.[65]

The financial benefits of being the chief remembrancer were notable. He was the one who collected debts due to the Crown, besides keeping the records of income and expenditure. The memoranda rolls found in this part of the Exchequer recorded investigations of financial irregularities, details of sheriffs' accounts, escheators' accounts, appointments of attorneys, orders for the seizure of property, inquisitions and grants of land, among other transactions.[66] The eighteenth-century legal historian referred to above, G.E Howard, described the post as the 'principal office of the court, of great trust'. As such, one could imagine that the opportunities for an unscrupulous operator to benefit from this were very numerous (though such things are almost never documented).[67]

One document in Robert's estate papers that is of particular historical note is his purchase of the pre-emption or 'reversion' of the post of chief remembrancer from Sir James Carroll. Carroll's letter, quoted below, is a relatively rare documented case of this practice. In 1630, obviously keen to put a stop to this tradition, Charles I sent a directive to the lord justices of Ireland, 'ordering them not to renew Robert Kennedy's patent of the offices of Remembrancer, or to give the office to anyone else upon Kennedy's surrender or death'.[68] This also included John, who evidently had engaged in a similar purchase. While not a direct reprimand of Robert, it would have cost him a large sum of money. He had paid nearly a thousand pounds for the post, and no doubt expected to sell it eventually for considerably more, or possibly pass it on to his son. The inclusion of documents pertaining to both Richard Colman's and Richard Hoper's appointments as chief remembrancers in 1609 and 1610 bears witness to Robert's penchant for record-keeping,[69] and perhaps to their own purchase of this post.

Just a year before his acquisition of the remembrancer's post, Robert had been co-opted onto a commission for the inquisition of some Wicklow land. The members of the commission were to be Sir Lawrence Esmond (whose family held Johnstown Castle in Wexford as well as Arklow Castle in the very south of County Wicklow as tenants of the Ormonds[70]), Sir William Brabazon (Earl of Meath), Sir Francis Annesley, Sir William Parsons, Sir Adam Loftus, William Barker, surveyor of the Court of Wards, William White, escheator of Leinster, Arthur Ussher and Scotsman Robert Pont, clerk and vicar of Rathdrum, Co. Wicklow (later murdered by some O'Byrnes[71]). Intriguingly, Robert Kennedy was deputised by Adam Loftus to function in his place.[72] Robert was obviously comfortable functioning at the highest levels, as this list includes some of the most important men in Ireland at the time.

Thus we see Robert Kennedy having reached the pinnacle of his progress in government posts. Aided by an education, his connection to Sir James Carroll had provided him with that all-important first step on the ladder of advancement. His personal ambition carried him forward to the notice of William Parsons, and from there to the highest circles of power in both the city and colonial governments. He had used his income to establish himself firmly as a man of importance in the City of Dublin. He owned a number of houses and dressed well. His coat of arms would have been emblazoned on all pertinent pieces of his property. Men of wealth at this time, however, were eager to have their large country estate, and Robert was no exception. A new decade continued to nurture his growing assets, which would allow him to acquire his much-sought-after estate.

2
Expanding

On every front, Robert Kennedy and his family were surging upwards in the race to wealth that was one of the main dynamics in the seventeenth century for well-connected entrepreneurs of the Protestant faith. His growing reputation and connection to high-ranking men on the Dublin scene helped him to secure options for property beyond Dublin. In this chapter we will look at other avenues by which Robert acquired increasing wealth and how he used this to expand his holdings and enhance his family. This occurred during the long stretch of peace between 1603, the end of the Nine Years War, and 1641, when Gaelic outrage over the extensive encroachment of English settlers and the English government into Irish life and land would explode.

One of the easiest sources of profit at this time was trading in King's Letters. These granted areas of Irish land which had been assessed at a specified sum. They had been given to favourites of the king, who would then sell them on, sometimes in lots of smaller portions. Those who purchased them could resell them in turn, a profit being made at each subsequent exchange. Landowners who only held their land at the pleasure of the king were left at the mercy of the king's whim. The fine print on the surrender and regrant agreements was beginning to bite.

As early as 1614 Robert Kennedy and William Rowlls had bought from David Roche, Viscount Fermoy, £17 worth of a £50 grant.[1] It had originally been given to the lord deputy, who obviously had then sold it on to Roche. In 1620 Robert, Rowlls and Henry Kenney were granted £43 worth of lands and rectories in Carlow and Cork by Thomas, Lord Cromwell, who had recently been granted them by James I.[2] The Carlow properties were passed along to Arthur Savage in 1621 by Robert, no doubt at a profit.[3] Lastly, in March 1627/8 Dudley Norton sold Robert £3 worth of a £100 grant that he had been given by Charles I.[4] Robert would have known Norton, as he was both chancellor of the Exchequer and secretary of state from 1612 to 1616.[5]

To increase the number of Protestants in the Irish parliament, many new boroughs were initiated by James I and Charles I. Only Protestants were eligible to apply to be a burgess, thus ensuring that the MPs from these sometimes-unsettled boroughs would be of the correct persuasion. In 1619 Robert had been named as a burgess in the establishment of the town of Newborough (now known as Gorey, Co. Wexford). He was to be one of twelve burgesses, with Sir Lawrence Esmond as the sovereign (head of the borough) and two commoners to do the work. The other burgesses included Thomas Ram, Bishop of Ferns, Sir Francis Annesley, Sir Adam Loftus, Sir James Ware and William Parsons.[6] There is no further documentation connecting Robert with Gorey, but as a burgess he would have had income from the renting of burgess plots and an interest in the commonage.[7] In years to come, the Kennedys would have more connections with other County Wexford people, particularly Matthew Ford, who became one of the guardians of Robert's great-grandsons.

In 1621 Robert and his brother John, likewise a legal clerk, acquired a number of parcels of land in the baronies of Granard and Longford, Co. Longford. In Robert's case, this was done by means of a trust for a local man, Connell McIrriell Ferrall.[8] The commission of 1622 called this 'a trick' that had circumvented the king's directive disbarring men from outside the county from getting such land. The entry also mentions that Robert Kennedy was a clerk to William Parsons,[9] which would indicate that he was double-jobbing, having been an Exchequer clerk at this time as well. The occurrence of William Parsons's name in both this activity and the Gorey enterprise would lead one to surmise that he was instrumental in the inclusion of Robert in these land deals. John Kennedy's descendants held onto his Longford lands even into the 1780s, as attested by later sources,[10] but Robert apparently sold his portion either to his brother or to someone else.

Another way in which money could be made was through the acquisition of plantation grants. These were freely given, costing the adventurer nothing but the effort of finding buyers. In April 1622 Robert Kennedy was given a royal grant for nearly 1,000 acres of land in Queen's County (Laois) for plantation. That demanded a rent of £5 per acre for 400 acres of pasture, and about half that for bogland and woods.[11] (Unusually, the grant in Latin still exists, as does Robert's sale of land to Peter Hussey in 1625, though they are not in his estate papers.[12]) This land was thus worth about £3,500. It would seem likely that it was the largest lot of property in Robert's land speculation efforts, likewise making the largest contribution to his finances. It was also his only royal grant.

Otherwise, the early 1620s continued to see more acquisitions, positions of influence and children becoming part of Robert's life. In 1622 he bought another house on St Nicholas Street,[13] as well as the Brownes' Kishoge mansion with 140 acres.[14] His daughter Mary was probably born in 1616,[15] his son Richard in 1623 and Thomas in 1625. In 1624 Robert was participating in the commission mentioned at the end of the last chapter, which was set up to decide whether or not more land should be confiscated in County Wicklow owing to the activities of Feagh McHugh O'Byrne in the previous century. An inquisition was duly held before a jury of both English and Gaelic men.[16] They found that the land in question had indeed belonged to this O'Byrne, who had been killed in rebellion in 1597. The confiscation went ahead and opened the way for the plantation of the Ranelagh area of County Wicklow.[17]

The remaining avenue of increasing his net worth, the buying of wardships, may have enabled Robert to make even bigger purchases in Wicklow. William Parsons (now Sir William) had been made master of the newly invigorated Court of Wards in 1622. This court required that, if a man's heir was not yet 21 years old when the man died, the heir would be made a ward of this court. This wardship was then sold to a relative or an investor. If the heir was not a Protestant, every effort would be made to require him to convert if he were to recover his estate. In the meantime, the one owning the wardship could sell whatever property he thought necessary in the ward's estate.

Robert took up this opportunity in 1623 and 1624 with the purchase of the wardships of Gerald Comerford in Kilkenny for £200 and Gilleduff McThomas O'Kelly of the Claddagh in Galway for £10.[18] The price of the wardship would have reflected the worth of the estate involved. The family of Gerald Comerford may have been known to Robert because Gerald had been one of the judges in the Exchequer in the early 1600s. He held extensive property in Kilkenny and had died in 1604 at around the age of 41. His eldest son, Fouke, died in 1623, and it is likely that Fouke's son was the subject of the wardship. The price of £200 would be suitable for the size of Gerald's holdings.[19] No documentation on Gilleduff McThomas appears to have survived.

Most propitiously, Robert's very wealthy cousin, Alderman Robert Kennedy, died at the end of 1624 with an underage heir.[20] This was an opportunity not to be missed, and Parsons would have ensured that our Robert bought this wardship.[21] Although its price was not recorded, it would have been substantial. Since the heir, John, was only nine months shy of his 21st birthday, Robert wouldn't have had a lot of time to asset-strip this very wealthy estate. His considerable experience in moving property would have served him well, however, and it could be surmised that not much was left to the heir apart from holdings in trusts.

In addition to this windfall, Margaret Sankey, widow of George Sankey, died the next year. She had made Robert her sole heir and executor, so he also came into George's estate. It would have been much more modest than that of the alderman, but it was no doubt very welcome in any event, including as it did leases for two houses, one of which was on St Nicholas Street. George had lived in it for 49 years.[22]

Curiously, with George Sankey's death, a court case was taken by a Thomas Hamlin, contending the ownership not only of his house but also of the property behind it, Jenefields Inns. In order to fund the case, Hamlin borrowed £50 via a mortgage from John Pue. In this way Pue came into ownership of both of these properties. There is no documentation of it, but Pue may have been acting on behalf of Robert Kennedy. Had Hamlin been doing the same? What is documented is that, just over a year later, Robert Kennedy is said to be in occupation of Jenefields Inns.[23] Further, John Pue was in fact Robert's brother-in-law, having married the second Sulliard daughter, Elizabeth.

The buildings were in poor condition, but Robert could see their potential. The original buildings were later demolished by this Kennedy family, who built a mansion on the site.[24] All these additional boons, along with his new post of chief remembrancer, would have greatly enhanced Robert Kennedy's coffers. It is only from this time that Robert started to spend large amounts of money in County Wicklow.

The situation of the landholders in Wicklow—and particularly in the O'Byrne's country, as it was known—was somewhat unusual. They had not been offered the option of 'surrender and regrant', which meant that they were freeholders. They did not hold their land at the pleasure of the king but as of tradition, 'time out of mind'. Nevertheless, they could still be impacted by King's Letters, whereby the king could bestow their land on someone else, as the king was the legal owner of all land in his kingdom. Fortunately, the original owners could buy it back, ostensibly for the cost of the documentation involved in so doing.

The head of a sept held the land of his sept, who were his extended family. They paid him a fee and he was expected to take care of them out of this income, but this fee was 'in kind'—that is, out of the produce of the land, not in cash. When the O'Byrne landholders had become 'gentlemen' in service to the government in Dublin as keepers of the peace in their area, including the barony of Rathdown, their lifestyle changed. They needed clothes that could not be made locally, as well as incurring other expenses that required cash. Moreover, County Wicklow had suffered harvest failures in the early years of the 1620s, and would again in the later years of this decade.[25]

All these changes would have increased the financial vulnerability of the freeholders in north Wicklow to proffered loans in the form of mortgages. Robert Kennedy would have known that, and he began to use this financial bind to gradually gain possession of the O'Byrne and O'Cullen lands. (The O'Cullens were the traditional physicians to the MacMurroughs, the traditional chiefs of Leinster. They held their land fee-free, but they likewise had started to acquire goods to enhance their standing that could only be bought for cash.)

Mortgages had been occurring among the O'Byrnes and the O'Cullens for some time, but only for a few pounds and perhaps a milk cow and her calf.[26] They were realistically repayable by the one taking the loan. There was, however, another way of manipulating property. Owing to the tradition of land being divided between all the male heirs of a landowner, many O'Byrnes had very small holdings. The practice of the more élite members of the clan was then to offer those smallholders, who had become distanced from the main blood line of the clan, more for their land than it was worth by means of a mortgage. In this way, these smallholders were unable to sell it to anyone else and the territory was consolidated and kept within the main body of the sept,[27] while the smallholder was reduced to the status of a tenant.

Given the background outlined above, circumstances had been generated for the acquisition of a large amount of land in Newcastle barony by a determined and astute Protestant Gaelic legal official by the name of Robert Kennedy. His mentor, William Parsons, modelled all the necessary character traits and behaviours needed to succeed in such a quest. Kennedy's rapid rise to power and property had been well orchestrated and is remarkable. His participation in the 1624 land commission gave him a much greater familiarity with County Wicklow, and the bowing out of a long-standing Wicklow seneschal of great political power (William Harrington) would have increased his freedom to function in the county. The Gaelic freehold landowners in Wicklow could see the writing on the wall: their ownership was under serious threat from an unscrupulous and single-minded government which used all avenues available to it to dispossess them. Their best option was to get what they could for their land.

The estate papers show that in the early 1620s other players were starting to engage with landowners in Newcastle parish. Farrell and Matthew O'Cullen had mortgaged the townland of Cooladoyle to Robert Clony for £250,[28] and followed it up with a Staple loan for £600.[29] Thomas FitzGerald of Dublin had given Edmond McJames O'Byrne of Kilmurry a mortgage for his land,[30] and Ralph Leventhorpe, also of Dublin, an MP for Ennis and an examiner for the Chancery, had given Farrell O'Cullen a mortgage for another one of his townlands.[31] A local man, Donogh McPhillip O'Clery of Killadreenan (descendant of a cleric of this church?), gave a mortgage to Shane McEnyer O'Byrne for part of yet another townland.[32] Farrell O'Cullen had been weakened by some of his land having been granted to Sir Lawrence Esmond by the king, which it then cost him to redeem.[33] If Robert Kennedy had not come into large amounts of money from 1625, would he have been able to outbid the rising tide of other investors?

Starting in 1626, Robert seized the opportunity of Farrell O'Cullen's financial distress and offered him a mortgage of £180 for a sizeable portion of his land.[34] This included a third of the townland of Ballygarny, which would become the central part of the Mount Kennedy demesne. (Remarkably, Robert had his eldest son, Sylvester, only eleven years old, witness this indenture.) In this document O'Cullen also acknowledged a previous Staple loan of £600, entered into with several other men.

Eleven months later, Robert waded in with even more money, over £738, and provided a joint mortgage to O'Cullen and Robert Clony, making it possible for O'Cullen to repay the Staple loan to Clony; Robert Kennedy was then financially in control of the land involved. This included the rest of O'Cullen's holdings, among which was the remaining two thirds of Ballygarny,[35] which would become Robert's sometime residence (see Illus. 10). The next day he rented O'Cullen's land back to him for 21 years. O'Cullen was unable to pay the rent and gave up his lease four years later.[36]

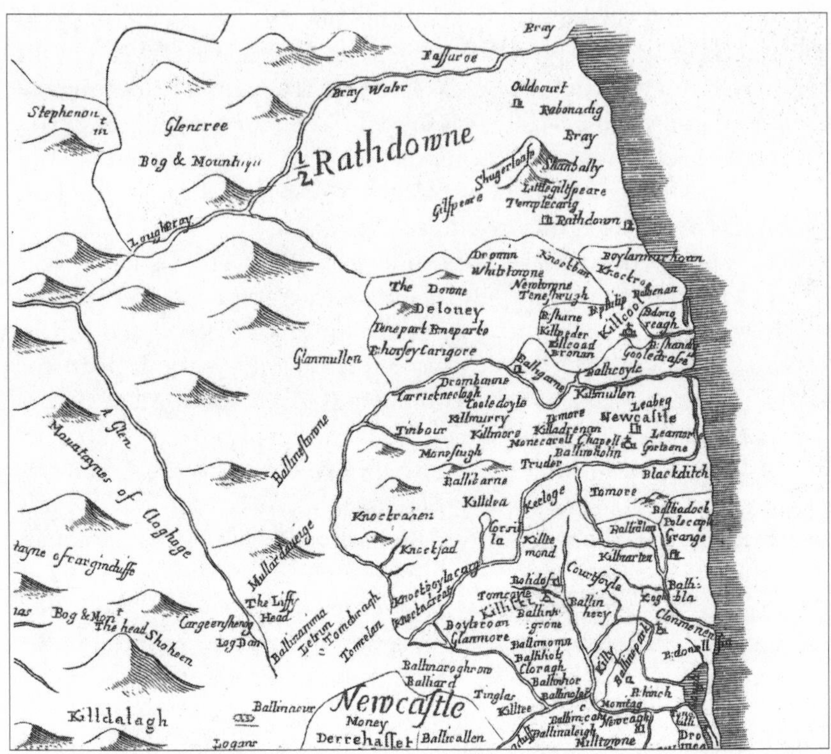

Illus. 10—Petty's 1685 map of Newcastle barony (TCD Maps Library, used with permission).

Robert continued his practice of renting the land of the Wicklow men back to them, which, one would imagine, engendered some anger. He charged them a specified rent for the first year, which was then increased for the following years. In addition, they were liable for all government taxes as well as two hens at Christmas and some days' work at jobs for him. This included such things as bringing in turf or mending watercourses and mills. Nor did they have access to the trees on the land, which Robert reserved to himself.[37]

Robert continued his gradual acquisition of land in Newcastle barony, buying some parcels outright and providing mortgages to others. Sometimes he continued to advance more and more money to the freeholder until repayment was guaranteed to be impossible. An example of the latter is his interaction with James O'Byrne, the owner of Ballynahinch (previously known as Ballymacandrick). The initial mortgage in late March 1631 was for £80.[38] In May Robert and James jointly rented it to Sanky Sulliard, apothecary (a brother-in-law of

Robert's), whereby James received £3 15*s* yearly while Robert got £4 5*s*.[39] In November of that year O'Byrne was given another £43, but this time Edmond Gerrott O'Byrne of Monalin was required to guarantee the loan.[40] In July 1633 he was given another £64. According to James himself, as of 30 June 1636,

> 'By my deed of the last of July 1633 I ... leased all my right, interest, conditions, or Limitations of use in the premises for the somme of £64 ... after which ... Robert Kennedy, upon my allogacon [allegation] to him that the Landes were more worth, gave unto me a note ... stating that if I did pay Robert £144 within six years ... Robert was by that note content to deliver me the Lande: which promise ... Robert made, for that ... Lande weare [were] not truly worth so much money as he disbursed ... which I finde to be true for that I have made offer of the sale of the premises to several able and likely persons who refused to deal therein by reason the money ... weare over greate and more then the Lande weare or are truly worth.'

James went on to sell his land to Robert Kennedy for an additional £5.[41]

James O'Byrne received £211 for nearly 1,500 acres. One could say that at least his ownership was not given to someone else through a royal grant, or confiscated. On the other hand, was the price he got for it fair? Either way, he was no longer a landowner but had become landless. What Robert had done here was to use the Gaelic élite's tool of consolidating a sept's landholdings. The difference is that James's land was not a smallholding, and he would only have continued access to what had been his land if he paid a significant yearly rent. This is not a sept consolidation; it is a stranger taking over what had been the traditional land of the O'Byrnes.

Over the second half of the 1620s and the first half of the 1630s, Robert Kennedy gradually bought out many of the freeholders in much of what would become upper Newcastle parish, and some in the parishes of Kilcoole and Killiskey, to the north and south respectively.[42] Ultimately, it included all the townlands in the shaded area on the map of the Kennedy estate (Illus. 11). Those townlands in bold italics were also acquired in this initial stage of expansion, but were sold at some point and are not listed in later details of the estate.

Recall that Robert Kennedy was no stranger in north County Wicklow since his marriage in 1614, which provided him with a family

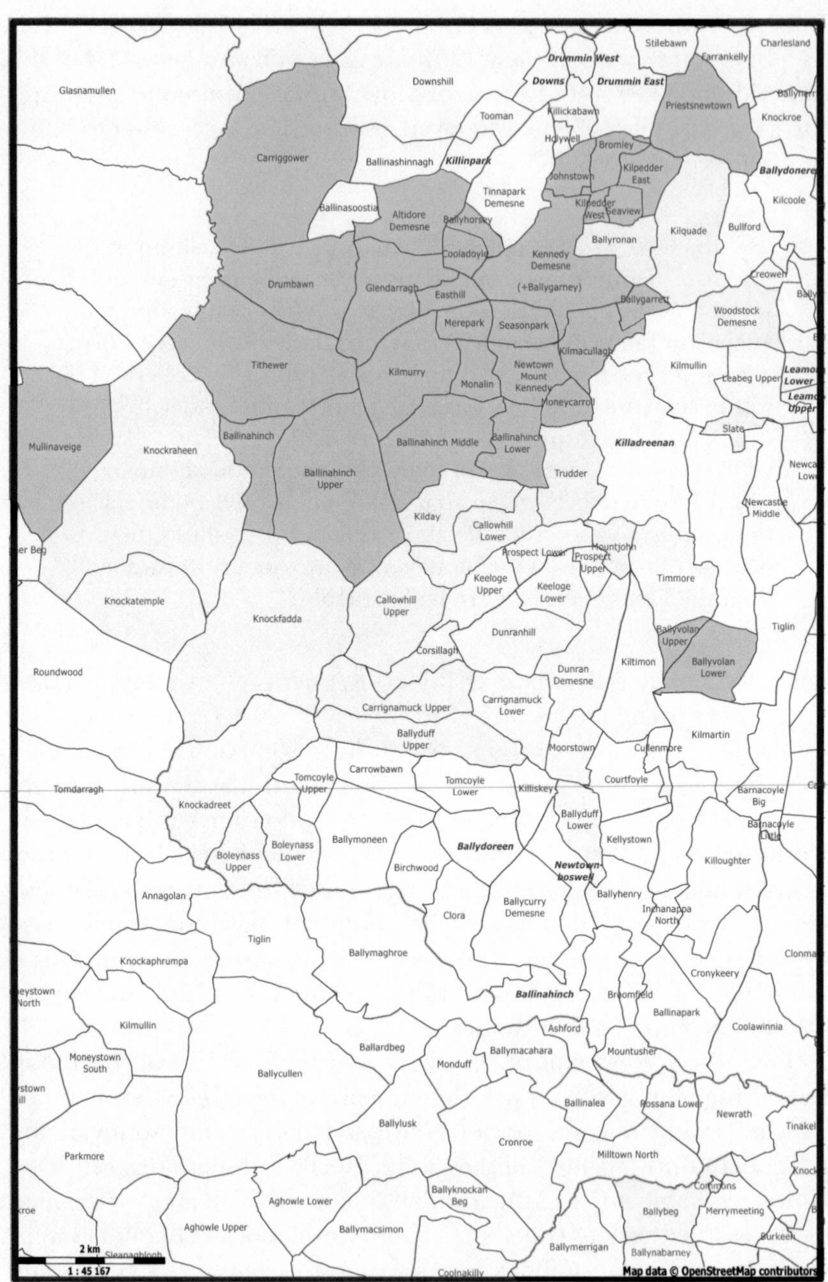

Illus. 11—Map of the Kennedy estate's townlands (drawn by Brian Hollinshead of Open Street Mapping).

connection to the Rathdown Talbots. Thinking him trustworthy, Peter Talbot had made him a trustee of his property, a position meant to safeguard it. Peter's death in 1622 allowed Robert to legally asset-strip the estate. Like most people who profit at someone else's expense, Robert was ruthless. Later, we will see how Bernard, Peter's heir, dealt with this betrayal of the family's trust.

Further, Robert would marry his eldest daughter to the eldest son of the Shanganagh Walshes in 1631. Their tower-house still stands. (Shanganagh is the area just north of Shankill, which in the seventeenth century was not the settlement that it is today.) These Walshes had extended family down the Wicklow coast, as well as one Walsh owning a townland, Tinnapark, just north of Robert's Newcastle parish holdings.

At this time Robert also continued to acquire more houses on St Nicholas Street[44] (at least one of which he had built[45]), and these provided rental income. In one 'cross-over' transaction, two O'Byrne men exchanged their land in Kilmurry for a house to live in on St Kevin Street in Dublin until they died.[46] Interestingly, Robert had bought that house from an O'Byrne living on St Bride's Street in Dublin.[47] (St Patrick Street was the continuation of St Nicholas Street beyond the gate of the city wall, whereas St Bride's Street was the next one parallel to the east, a continuation of St Werburgh's Street.) The O'Byrne presence in Dublin would be consistent with their long-time support of the English government and their status as 'gentlemen'.

Robert had accumulated enough money to acquire townlands in County Wicklow. He had ready money, the fruit of his prior land speculation and his ongoing exploitation of underage heirs. One of the commodities most coveted by the wealthy of the time was their own estate. This meant amassing land (generally contiguous), its being made a manor by the king and the owner granted a title. Often this land would be obtained through a royal grant, but Robert didn't have those kinds of connections. What he did have was knowledge of how land was acquired, how it could be made vulnerable through financial instruments, and how men could be manipulated with warmth and promises. To help him safeguard his activity in gaining land in this county, Robert Kennedy set up a trust of very influential men, as previously described.

Gradually moving his way up in the Court of the Exchequer and with networking, he attained the highest clerical office in that court, the chief remembrancership. It would be hard to know whether his brother John, still a Catholic, would have been able, or would have wanted, to exercise any moderating influence. Bribes would have continued apace, along with other perks. Robert was able to make good use of the opportunities, and his cultivation of the 'right people' paid off handsomely.

Given that they were the group under strong political and financial pressure in this period, it is tempting to think of Catholics as honest, or at least law-abiding, but there is ample evidence that religion was irrelevant when it came to matters of business and professional promotion. Even those Catholics who went to prison for their faith were known to be involved in shady dealing. There is documentation that Alderman Robert Kennedy was involved in currency speculation.[48] It is just as likely that John Kennedy was as comfortable as Robert with dishonest dealings.

The social implications of this rapid rise in the law and landownership were significant. Robert's purchase of the Browne estate with a mansion in Kishoge gave him the means of establishing his rank within the Dublin hierarchy by having a country residence, a major status symbol. In 1626 Robert had been admitted to the professional body of lawyers, the King's Inns, as a 'member', indicating that he was of sufficient standing to gain this distinction.[49] He had much of the wealth of Alderman Robert Kennedy, the Sankey estate, money from asset-striped wardships and the chief remembrancer's post, making him wealthier than he could ever have reasonably expected to be.

Further consequences of acquiring this amount of property can be seen in the opportunities availed of by his children. The records of Trinity College tell us that two of Robert's sons attended there. Sylvester had given an engraved cup to the college *c.* 1630 as he was moving on to his legal training at Lincoln's Inn. This is scant information, as is typical for the records of their early attenders. Sylvester would have been fifteen at this point. On the same page, his brother Thomas has a similar entry in the record, noting that there was 'brought in [on] June 8 1635 … Thos. Kenedye's beaker'.[50] Thomas would have been, at most, eleven that year, so it is difficult to know at what level he had received his education. He does not appear to have gone on to Lincoln's Inn, according to extant records.

Trinity College would only have been in existence for 38 years when Sylvester donated the cup, and simply having attended would have been a rare privilege. If we assume that Sylvester was around twelve when he started, his year of admission would have been 1627. Thomas probably followed in 1632. James Carroll, as Trinity's treasurer, may well have facilitated the admission of Robert's sons.[51] While there, they would have rubbed shoulders with many boys who would later become important and powerful men. It was their entry into the 'old boys' network'.

What is interesting is that Robert's second son, Richard, does not appear to have attended Trinity (though it is not impossible, as the state of TCD records at this point was very poor), yet both he and Sylvester went on to Lincoln's Inn in London. Lincoln's Inn has confirmed that Sylvester was admitted there in March 1630/1. Richard was admitted in August 1638, which indicates a seven- or eight-year gap in their ages. Another piece of the family legal portrait is the page for Kennedys in the King's Inns' Black Book. Richard and Thomas both became members of this august institution in January 1656/7. (Sylvester had died before this date.[52]) They were obviously well accepted by the legal establishment of their day.

Kennedy's entrance into well-to-do circles of Irish society is also reflected in the marriages of his daughters. Two entries in the *Calendar of Inquisitions*[53] attest to the fact that Robert was able to provide his daughter Mary with a dowry of £800 in 1631. This was a very large sum of money at the time and demonstrates how wealthy he had become. The other interesting aspect of this marriage is that he chose to marry her into an old Cambro-Norman Catholic family, the Walshes of Shanganagh, to John, son of James. These Walshes were also related to the O'Tooles and the O'Byrnes (as well as the Walshes of Carrickmines), which would have established links to these two important Wicklow families.[54]

Robert's second daughter, Bridget, had married Michael Doyne in 1650. The Doynes were similarly a legal family, Gaelic and Anglicised. Her son, Robert Doyne, eventually became the chief justice of the Court of the Exchequer in 1695 and chief justice of the Court of Common Pleas in 1703, even though his father had died in 1654 and Bridget had remarried.[55]

The last of Robert's daughters, Catherine, probably born around 1638 (roughly 23 years after Sylvester), married Thomas, the son of Robert Burdett, a London merchant and alderman, whose wife likewise came from the family of a London alderman. In 1630 the king had granted Burdett twenty townlands in County Carlow, centred around Leighlin and Leighlin Bridge, the stronghold of the MacMurroughs, once kings of Leinster. This Kennedy/Burdett liaison would have extended Robert's networking circle into the next county, as well as giving him undoubtedly useful connections to London merchants. Robert Burdett and Catherine married in 1653, and the heir was born in 1668. It is possible that Burdett had returned to London with the outbreak of the 1641 rebellion, which would account for the late marriage.[56]

Robert Kennedy obviously had money to spend, but he had the unfortunately common habit of not repaying his debts. At the beginning of 1632, there is an acknowledgement in his papers of money owing to his brother Walter. Robert had written out a simple IOU, specifying the sum as £24 10*s*. Walter proceeded to add, under Robert's signature, 'the summe of £24 10*s* above is over and above the summe of £150 15*s* and use [interest] that my brother is owing to me'.[57] All the while, Robert was spending money on land acquisition, not something that would have amused his creditors.

Sir James Carroll was not going to make the same mistake twice of forgiving Robert his debts. Just before Christmas 1632, he sent Robert a letter requiring repayment of £157 15*s* 6*d* which had been outstanding for seven years:

> 'I prai you take this accompt [account] into consideration and give me satisfaction for it. You know that what I did for you in it was my love to you and your wife more than the espect [expectation] of gaine that I might have had from another, as you well know, and therefore I hope that you will not cause me [to] suffer for anie summe that remains of the small price that I sold the office to you. I am unwilling to speake or urge much where I do affect, and believe that I am affected and desire to avoid all occasions of unkindness. I am now to leave the towne and therefor I pray you to send me £20 by the bearer or what you can well spare and let the remaine[der] rest till my return & that we all agree on the accompt [account].'[58]

He continued to sign himself 'your loving Cossen Ja Carroll', but surely there is a bit of displeasure at having been taken advantage of. Nevertheless, we can see from this letter that Robert's wife was socially active with him. The very sensitive phrasing of the letter also demonstrates the great contrast between Carroll's private life and the very sharp business practices in which he engaged. These would later make him a target for a crusading lord deputy.

It is not clear from whom Kennedy might have borrowed any money that he needed to bankroll his Wicklow investments. We have evidence that he had borrowed from his brother Walter and James Carroll. The Statute Staple, which would have been another option, shows only three uses of the Staple by this Robert Kennedy, all of them as a lender rather than a borrower. The first two of these were prior to his Wicklow activities, in 1620 and 1625, and were to people outside of Wicklow, in Kildare/Kilkenny and Meath. It was only in 1634 that he lent £1,200 to Edmond O'Byrne of Tinnaparke (a townland just north of his then current acquisitions) via the Staple.[59] (This O'Byrne was related to Robert's daughter Mary's husband, one of the Shanganagh and Killincarrig Walshes.)[60] Other possibilities are that his income from the Exchequer and the Kennedy wardship were very substantial, or he could have been accessing money via the Exchequer system.

In 1634 Robert was able to refer to himself as 'Robert Kennedy of Ballygarny'.[61] There must therefore have been a residence on the townland, most likely a tower-house, as there is later evidence of one that stood on a pre-existing motte.[62] It is difficult to know when this defensive structure was built. The O'Byrnes were known to be building their own defences possibly as early as the fifteenth century but there

Illus. 12—Detail from a 1680 map by Nicholas Visscher (courtesy of the Barry Lawrence Ruderman Collection).

Illus. 13—Detail of John Rocque's 1760 map of Ireland (David Rumsey Map Collection, David Rumsey Map Center, Stanford Libraries (https://www.davidrumsey.com/maps2576.html); accessed 28 January 2022).

are no references to a tower-house in Ballygarny in O'Byrne or O'Cullen records,[63] so it is likely that it was built in the 1620s by Robert himself after he bought it from Farrell O'Cullen. The motte would have been erected at the time of the Anglo-Normans, and a wooden structure erected on it. As was typical, it was built at a river crossing, which allowed for the control of traffic in the area as well as the construction of a mill. Then workers' cottages were built alongside the river, constituting the 'new town'.[64] A tower-house was definitely out of fashion by the 1620s but it would have been secure. Still, it was obviously less commodious than Robert's house in Dublin or his mansion in Kishoge and he is unlikely to have spent much of his time there.

An interesting query concerns the route that Robert would have taken when making his way to his Wicklow holdings. Early maps of this area rarely detail the roads, but Nicholas Visscher II, a Dutch cartographer, in his 1680 map, *Regnum Hiberniae*, did include the north/south road through the barony of Rathdown, the coast road running through Bray and Newcastle (Illus. 12).[65] Some of Kennedy's interaction with the O'Byrnes and the O'Cullens may have occurred at the local administrative centre of Newcastle McKynegan. His relatives at Rathdown would have provided him with lodgings on his trips to the county, but at some point he would have ridden over to Ballygarny. A much later map (John Rocque's of 1760, published in 1790) shows that there was a definite road that ran from Red Ford (just north of present-day Greystones, so called because of the colour of the local stone) to Delgany, and from thence to Mount Kennedy (Illus. 13). No doubt there were many local trails that had been used for centuries, but this route would evidently have been a much-used one in order for it to appear on a map. Only roads that carried 'through traffic', i.e. to Wexford and Waterford, were of interest to the map-makers' purchasers. Both these maps, of course, only appeared a number of decades after Robert Kennedy's time.

In this chapter, covering the 1620s up to the mid-1630s, we have seen how Robert Kennedy, making use of his networks and government offices, accessed other avenues of income and used these to acquire the land that would become his manor. He impressed those around him as a very astute and clever operator in dealing with property. 'Providence' continued to smile on him and circumstances conspired to make it possible for him to gain the necessary land. It seemed that he was well on his way to joining the ranks of the most influential men of his day, many of whom had used his services in interactions that provided mutual benefit.

3
Decades of turmoil

In 1633 the Irish government and men of power were confronted by the force that was Thomas Wentworth (Illus. 14). He had been a zealous reformer in the north of England, driven to make local functionaries subject to the law of the land by suppressing local advantages. While this had made him very unpopular with the local élites, he had gained the favour of the king, who was reaping the benefits of Wentworth's efforts. His career ostensibly progressed when he was appointed lord deputy of Ireland and arrived in July of that year. Wentworth was determined to eliminate the self-aggrandising practices of the Protestants who ran the government there in order to enhance the king's coffers (as well as his own). To this end, he began calling the powerful to task and challenging their privileges. He was particularly hostile to William Parsons, whom he would have seen, correctly, as one of the worst offenders against the public—read the king's—good. He was able to gain most of Parsons's holdings in County Wicklow for himself (land that was later part of the Fitzwilliam estate, Wentworth's eventual heirs).

With his self-described 'thoroughness', he also pursued the lower-ranking men in Parsons's circle. Records show that on 20 May 1634 a warrant was issued firing Robert Kennedy from his post as the chief remembrancer of the Court of the Exchequer (and John as well, though he is not mentioned in this warrant).

> 'Whereas by reasons of manifold misdemeanours and abuses committed by Robert Kennedy in the execution of the place or office of chief remembrancer to his Majesty in his Highness's Court of Exchequer, he the said Kennedy being fairly proceeded against and questioned for the same was found and so censured to be a man unworthy of the place and employment ...'[1]

Illus. 14—Portrait of Thomas Wentworth.

At around 50 years of age, after a lifetime as a court official, Kennedy had been unceremoniously booted from his place of power.

One of the amazing things about British bureaucracy is the amount of material that has been preserved. The downside of this is the difficulty of finding the particular document that is needed—or even of knowing that it exists. By great good luck, the search engines threw up an unexpected treasure. There is no date on the document, but it was probably written sometime after Wentworth was executed in 1641 and before Charles I suffered the same fate in 1649. Robert Kennedy had petitioned Parliament for the restoration of himself and his brother John to the office of the chief remembrancer. Far from being a mundane listing of supporting evidence that would bolster his case, the document describes in vivid detail the total travesty of justice that was Wentworth's trademark.

'The humble Petition of Robert and John Kennedy Esqr' is the first of two sections. The opening page is addressed to Parliament, outlining the Kennedys' history in the post; it then asserts that they were illegally deprived of the office so that three of Wentworth's friends could benefit from the profits thereof. The second part is a declaration providing the gruesome details of what was done by Wentworth and his friends to achieve their ends.

It begins with the fact that Kennedy was not allowed to consult with any legal counsel in dealing with the charges against him. The jury was only given the evidence verbally by the prosecutor. No written copy was produced for their examination until the inquisition was finalised. When Kennedy tried to question the lack of proof for some of the charges, the meeting was adjourned and moved to another venue, from which Kennedy was barred. Only Wentworth's friends were allowed in. When the jury baulked at this, the session was again adjourned; they were still given no copy of the charges. They met two days later and were told that if they did not confirm the charges they would be imprisoned in Dublin Castle. Kennedy then brought charges of jury intimidation in the court of the Chancery against the sergeant who had delivered this threat. At this point Wentworth put Kennedy in the Castle gaol and told him that he would not be let out until he begged forgiveness from the sergeant on his knees in Chancery. Kennedy had no option but to comply with Wentworth's demand. When the jury commenced again, they were told not to give heed to anything that Kennedy said in his defence. Before the day of his defence, Kennedy had been dispossessed of his office and found guilty of having falsified records in his office. In the meantime, several men had searched Kennedy's office for evidence but had found none.

Another tactic that Wentworth used was to imprison Kennedy and all his clerks, pressuring them for confessions. Two of the clerks mentioned some of their own oversights, whereby they had not given appropriate advantage to some people who had come before the Exchequer court. These relatively small details were seized upon and used as the pretext for Kennedy's dismissal, depriving him of his lifetime appointment.

One of Wentworth's men, Wandesford, a Chancery judge, subsequently received half of Kennedy's office and sold it for £900; the other two men in Wentworth's service each received a quarter of the office. Furthermore, Kennedy reported that he had evidence that Wandesford, before coming to Ireland, had made a deal with a man to give him £300 a year if he would deliver the office of chief remembrancer to him. This clearly demonstrated that the plot to unseat Kennedy had been a long time in motion. Another man had told Kennedy that Wentworth had given his word to people whom Kennedy knew well that he would not be put out of office unless there were evidence of major wrongdoing.

Two and a half years later, Wentworth and his men had told Kennedy that if he paid £2,000 his son Sylvester could have Kennedy's former office. Kennedy gave them the first of two instalments, but it was given back after five months, at least with interest. There were no further offers for the recovery of what had been brutally stolen from him. Later, Kennedy offered to show how he had called in debts to the Crown that were 40 or 50 years old, netting £12,000, but Wentworth dismissed this as irrelevant.[2]

Such a recitation of wrongdoing illustrates very powerfully how government functioned in Dublin. It was strictly a case of might making right. Kennedy himself was no angel and would have engaged in similar strong-arm tactics. These would have been a very traumatic few months for him, threatening both his financial security and his bodily survival. His efforts to recoup his post, making use of a fight response, would have eased the after-effects to some degree. The support of his family, and his then young adult sons, may have been instrumental in his continued struggle.

Despite suffering such a severe blow, Kennedy was apparently able to weather the financial storm that his loss of employment would have triggered. His estate papers attest that he continued to consolidate his landholdings in County Wicklow. This involved acquiring some of the remaining parcels within townlands like Drummin, Monalin and Kilmacullagh,[3] of which he already owned the major part. He also lent Edmond O'Cullen small sums of money over several months, part of the strategy of putting the owner in debt to the point where he would have to forfeit his land.[4] The most notable of his transactions between 1634 and 1639 was his exchange of properties with William Parsons. Kennedy gave Parsons land around Dunganstown in the Arklow barony, and in return he received parts of Kilmurry, Kilday and Killadreenan, which were much closer to Ballygarny.[5]

By this time, of course, Kennedy would also have developed quite an extensive network of business contacts. As an officer of the Exchequer, and especially as the chief remembrancer, he would have come into contact with many of the men conducting property transactions throughout the country. Richard Boyle, Earl of Cork, was one of these. Boyle kept diaries of his business (and other) activities;

these still survive. From them we see that he first interacted with Robert Kennedy in 1620, when he was then the chief chamberlain. Initially, Boyle is seen paying the fees owed for his transactions. Later, however, Kennedy appears to be acting as a financial intermediary for Boyle, holding accounts for collection, receiving the money and passing it on to Boyle. Was this an official function or business on the side, performing a service as a private operator?[5]

Kennedy's most extensive interaction with Boyle concerned some of the lands of Baltinglass Abbey, Co Kildare. This property had a complex ownership history in the 1620s. At some point James Carroll had gained an interest in them via a trust of which Robert Kennedy and John King were the trustees. Carroll and others had then taken out a mortgage on them. The mortgage was about to be defaulted upon when, on the last possible day in November 1629, Boyle had borrowed money and redeemed the mortgage for himself. Over the next few years he had cleared all the other interests on the property and was ready to receive his due title. On 22 March 1635, when Kennedy was no longer employed at the Exchequer, what looks like a very sociable meeting took place:

> 'Mr Robert Kennedy, by the direction and in the presence of Sir James Carroll, did this day promise me in my gallery, that he would conveigh & Releas unto me, the ... parcels of Th[e]abbey of Baltinglas, and ... Sir James Carroll; who with his Ladie, Mr Kennedy, & his wyffe, ar[e] to pass me a ffyne therof the next tearm.'[7]

Here is clear evidence that Kennedy's position within the circle of financial élites of the 1630s was well secured. The location of this gathering would have been at Cork House. Boyle had bought the twelfth-century church of Sante Marie del Dam, just outside the gate of Dublin Castle, in 1600. He then proceeded to demolish it, and build himself a fine townhouse on the site. (The street in front of it and alongside, leading up to the Castle, became known as Cork Hill, now the location of the City Hall. The church gave its name to Dame Street.) The Earl of Cork had a reputation for destroying church buildings.[8]

The financial impact of the loss of Kennedy's post would have been softened to some extent by the marriage of his eldest son, Sylvester, to Mary Crofton in May 1636.[9] She brought with her lands and money as befitted the daughter of William Crofton of Temple House, Co. Sligo, then the auditor-general (and thus Kennedy's former boss). Hopes were high that a prosperous dynasty of many generations was getting under way. If Kennedy had not lost his post, one wonders whether he could have sourced an even more prestigious woman.

Kennedy's loss of his job would have had a major impact on his cash flow. In December 1636 he was trying to pay off a loan from his brother Walter by assigning him a monthly payment from some of his rental income.[10] In November 1637 his brother John agreed to stand surety for him because he owed £400 to James Pollexfin of Dublin.[11] These financial pressures are just the ones for which records still exist. Others took him to court to try to extract their money (more of which later).

His second son, Richard, started in Lincoln's Inn in 1638, which would have required money for tuition, lodgings and maintenance. At around this same time his eldest son, Sylvester, had finished at the same institution. Apparently, Sylvester did not take up any court post but probably would have established himself in private practice, aided by his father's network. It would not be unreasonable to assume that some of Sylvester's income would have gone to his father, perhaps in the form of rent for one of the houses owned by Kennedy on St Nicholas Street. Another possibility is that, after their firing, Robert and John Kennedy had set up their own consultancy offices for legal advice and perhaps something akin to lobbying. Neither of them had attended an Inns of Court and technically they would not have been able to act as attorneys.

When Sylvester came back from Lincoln's Inn as a trained barrister, they would then have been able to offer services at that level. Kennedy's other sons, Richard (after his training at Lincoln's Inn) and Thomas (trained in-house?), may well have joined them. John had at least four adult sons by this time and perhaps one or two of these may also have entered the family practice. The firm would have been a formidable nexus of legal skills and networking. Another significant contributor to Kennedy's cash flow would have been his agricultural projects on his Ballygarny property, as we shall see.

Not long after Kennedy's loss of office, Sir James Carroll was ousted from his office of mayor of Dublin in 1635 and imprisoned at the insistence of Wentworth for price-gouging on coal-trading. He had been caught selling coal for twice the amount that he had paid for it.[12] With such intense political storms roiling in the capital, Robert Kennedy could have decided to keep his head down and retire to his Ballygarny and Kishoge estates. On the other hand, he may, like his brother John,[13] have reverted to the post of second chamberlain of the Exchequer, to which he still held the entitlement. The loss of status which this would have entailed might have been more than he could stomach, however, and he may have employed a deputy instead.

Next, Kennedy began to find himself the object of court cases, something from which he would have been immune as an Exchequer official. The first of the cases to come against him of which we are aware is that of Paul Harris. Harris is someone about whom we know quite a lot. He was an English Catholic priest who had opted into the Irish Catholic diocese of Meath. He was a contentious character who was quite vocal in the battle between diocesan priests like himself (known as 'seculars) and priests who were members of religious communities (known as 'regulars' because they were regulated by a rule of life) for the money given by lay Catholics for the administration of the sacraments.[14] This case appears to have been a fight over such clerical income between Harris and Kennedy. It was quite common for Catholics to make financial provisions in their will for a certain number of Masses to be said for their soul, as well as money given to the poor and prisoners to say prayers for the same purpose. This was true of John Browne.

The background to the case is as follows. John Browne had taken a 61-year lease on the church lands of Balgaddy in 1615. After a few decades, the value of the lands had improved and thus the rent was increased by the Anglican archbishop. As so often happened in this period of time, the rights to the site were passed along in a series of deals to increase income for each successive person. John Browne had demised this Balgaddy land to a Joseph Browne at a higher price, while at the same time selling the reversion, or the right to take on the lease when it became available, to William Turnor. Joseph Browne had in turn assigned or sold his rights to the land to Robert Kennedy. Thus Kennedy was initially paying his rent to Joseph Browne.[15]

At this point there is no mention of payment of tithes, and it may be that church officials had lost track of these tithes, sometimes listed as 'concealed' in church records.[16] Kennedy's acquisition probably occurred sometime after 1626, when he was actively pursuing land. When John Browne died, again probably in the early 1630s, his will took effect, which meant that money then had to be given to a priest (or priests) for the prayers required in the will, as well as to William Turnor, who took over the lease. Paul Harris was evidently the priest who was given the job of saying the Masses and distributing money to the praying poor. When the archbishop increased the rent, Harris evidently insisted that more money was due to him as well.

This very complex case is made more difficult to understand because, while we have the recommendation of the court for this first stage of the fight between Harris and Kennedy, we do not have either the initial complaint made by Harris or the one made by Kennedy two or three years later. What we do know is that in 1636 Harris took a case in civil court against Kennedy to demand that he be paid an additional sum. Harris won his case and Kennedy began paying the higher amount.[17] Receipts dated between 1636 and 1638 still exist, documenting his payment.[18] After a couple of years Kennedy evidently stopped paying the increased contribution to Harris. It would seem that Harris then went to the Protestant Bishop John Bramhall of Derry and made a complaint to him, though on what grounds is unclear, as Harris was not receiving tithes, which would have been under Bramhall's jurisdiction.[19] It could be that Harris had somehow managed to get Kennedy to pay him the tithes that should have been going to the archbishop. Whatever the details of the situation, Kennedy found himself imprisoned on foot of a Bramhall order.

Kennedy then took a case against Harris in 1639, maintaining that he had been locked up because Harris had lied to Bramhall.[20] At this point Wentworth, on Sir George Radcliffe's (a close friend of Wentworth's and a member of the Irish privy council) recommendation, allowed Kennedy his freedom after he posted a £40 bond in order to go and have a word with Bramhall. Perhaps in anticipation of the outcome of Radcliffe's recommendation, Kennedy had a receipt for a payment to the archbishop of Dublin, dated 22 May 1639, covering the period from the end of September 1637 to Easter 1639. This may well have been for the relevant tithes. It may have been this document that persuaded Bramhall not to continue Kennedy's imprisonment when they met, sometime after 3 August.[21] Wentworth, Bramhall's chief supporter and enforcer, was recalled to England that September, however, and there are no more receipts from the archbishop (or Harris). Wentworth was beheaded in 1641. As one can see from this Kennedy/Harris example, land transactions, politics and church matters were tightly interwoven, making any court cases involving them a veritable maze of rights and entitlements and devilishly difficult to disentangle.

What is most puzzling about this case, however, is why Paul Harris, a Catholic priest, was entertained at all by the court. While it is true that he was basing his case on the provisions of a will, the State did not recognise the services for which he was claiming increased recompense. Even more amazing, then, is that he won his case and that Kennedy paid up. There are two possibilities that could explain this. One is that Harris, who was a thorn in the side of the friars of Dublin (one of whom was the Catholic archbishop of Dublin), was being supported by the court in order to give him more political weight and thus exacerbate the internal distress of Catholic institutions in Ireland.[22]

The other possibility is more startling. It would suggest that Robert Kennedy was himself a radical Protestant. The government would be inclined, especially under Wentworth, to undermine the fortunes of radical Protestants, who were starting to challenge the king's privileges and status. If Kennedy had been an Established Church Protestant, it is more likely that the court would not have taken the case, or would have found against Harris. Given the severely anti-Catholic *and* anti-Gaelic stance of radical Protestants, Kennedy's own alienation from his family and the Roman Catholic Church might have been passionate. One can only wonder what the back-story to his conversion had been. If this was indeed the case, it would fit very well with many more of the details of Kennedy's life. It would sit quite comfortably with his level of integration into William Parsons's circle, to which the records testify. It could explain his marriage to a woman whose brother would become the mayor of Dublin under the Cromwellians, as well as his son Richard's enlistment in a Parliamentarian regiment and marriage to a woman from a radical English Protestant family.

It might be useful to look at what in radical Protestantism might have attracted the young Robert Kennedy to its ranks. While the radicals had initially focused on ritual reform—that is, how the priest or minister dressed and what prayers were said at a service—they had gradually also begun to demand that a sermon be preached so as to inspire and instruct the laity. They were very critical of corruption among the Anglican bishops, not to mention the Roman Catholics. Further, they began to consider themselves 'the godly', viewing all other Christians as 'ungodly' owing to their lack of a conversion experience.[23]

The young are noted for their idealism, and for their critical approach to their elders who have long since lost theirs. Yet the times were very Machiavellian, and idealism can quickly turn to cynicism. Kennedy may well have seen that there were no saints among his elders, but the radical Protestants had constructed a powerful and extensive network among themselves. If nothing else, they were getting ahead at the expense of all the others. He may also have been persuaded by their preachers once he had opted into their religious services and Bible reflection groups, and may possibly have undergone a conversion. Their sense of being holier than all other sects of Christianity may have promoted his high-handed dealings with others not of his persuasion. Nevertheless, whether it was conviction or pragmatism that led Kennedy to make his choice of churches, that choice served him well for the next 60 years.

Gilbert, in his *History of the City of Dublin*, provides many interesting details about life in Dublin down through the centuries. These include some interesting characters who appeared on the social scene from time to time and won acceptance at the highest levels. One such fellow, relevant to the intricacies of interaction between the government and Catholics, was Sir Toby Matthews. Quoting a hostile source, Gilbert writes:

> 'In March, 1639, the Earl of Strafford carryed with him into Ireland Sir Toby Matthews, a notorious, pernicious English jesuited priest (banished at the beginning of this Parliament upon the importunity of both Houses), lodged this priest over against the Castle of Dublin, the house where the Earl did himself reside, and from whence this priest daily rode to publique masse-houses in Dublin, and negotiated the engaging of the Papists of Ireland in the war against Scotland.'[24]

Matthews was the eldest son of the erudite and witty Anglican archbishop of York, but had become a Catholic and was ordained a priest in 1614. He was so charismatic that he charmed everyone he met, and made very powerful friends. This included James I, who knighted him for his assistance in negotiating with the Spanish court. Any friend of James's was a friend of Wentworth's, and Matthews was welcomed at all social gatherings. He engaged men in conversation and reported all relevant information back to the Jesuits, with whom he was favourably connected. Thus religion was no obstacle if you were so socially acceptable that your presence was considered a boon to any gathering. This gives us some insight into how complex life was in the first half of the seventeenth century in matters of religion.

At the same time that Robert Kennedy was dealing with Paul Harris, he was also in court with one of his Wicklow mortgagees, Farrell

O'Cullen, a Gaelic gentleman. O'Cullen had apparently looked to Kennedy in the same way that Kennedy had looked to William Parsons—that is, as a promoter and protector—but in 1637 he began to realise that Kennedy's earlier promises would not be fulfilled. On 5 July a petition was put before Wentworth laying out O'Cullen's case:

> 'Robert Kennedy Esq hear[d] [I] had mortgaged to Robte Clooney … 3000 acres good Land, arable and pasture. [He,] unknown to [me,] purchased Clooney's interest and knowing [me] to be in want of moneyes offered to give [me] £60 more … [for] Certaine Lands in the countie which [he] promised and undertook that both himself and his Feofees should make good to [me and my] heires for ever as by his deed bearing date the 6th of October 1630 … Kennedy promised at any tyme upon demand to give [me] £300 at 5 per cent for and towards any purchase he could make, and that hee would take and accept [my] eldest Sonn, and breed him as carefully and tenderly as his owne both at school and else wheare, and accept him as his owne Sonn, make him one of his Clearkes in his office (hee being then the kings cheife Remembrancer in the Exchequer), and would be such a friend to [me] and [my] children as he never would see [me] or [my] children to want or bee unprovided for as the witnesses then present will justifie … [T]heise faire inticeing promises [of] which he hath not performed any parte [despite] being often thereto demanded. Kennedy soe circumvented [me] as [I] hath got an assurance from [him,] of [my] Lands being worth at least £300 and hath made an insufficient and fraudulent Convenance of [my] Lands in Exchange[,] the most parte of them being not [my] own but others proper Inheritance; and kept [away] from [me] soe as [I] could neither get Lands, possession or parcel thereof haveing earnestly sent[,] since that contract desired true and reall confirmation of the deed of Exchange.
>
> …
>
> May it please your Lordship to command the said Robte Kennedy forthwith to … performe his agreement and promises in regard hee hath gotten [my] whole estate into his hands whereby [me, my] wife and 13 orphans are utterly undone.'[25]

This plea lays out quite starkly the sort of deceit practised by Kennedy to beguile the local landholders into signing contracts under false pretences. Kennedy's reply to O'Cullen was simply to deny that he did or said any of what O'Cullen reported[26] (see Illus. 1). One might argue another interpretation of what happened here. It could be that Kennedy had originally intended to do what O'Cullen described in terms of taking care of him and his sons but his fall from employment then made it impossible for him to fulfil his commitments. He dealt peremptorily with O'Cullen to cover his inability to take care of himself, let alone someone who had been looking to him for patronage. Either way, Kennedy got more land and O'Cullen became landless.

This alternate interpretation is harder to defend, however, in light of a case taken by Bernard Talbot in May 1638. Kennedy had been appointed one of the trustees of Bernard's father, Peter. This is the same Pierce Talbot who was a brother-in-law of Robert Kennedy through his wife's family. On Peter's death in 1622, Kennedy had taken his estates and children into his custody and proceeded to asset-strip and take the rents, amounting in total to nearly £1,200. In rebuttal, Kennedy claimed that his taking care of the family had cost him more than £1,200.[27] The number of children involved was only five. The court directed that accountants be employed to calculate whether the sum that Kennedy was claiming to have spent was a reasonable one, but it would seem unlikely that such a large sum could have been expended in meeting the needs of this family.

As with his earlier investments in wardships, it would seem more likely that Kennedy was mercenary and ruthless with vulnerable families, even when they were closely related to him. On the other hand, these Talbots were dispossessed by the Cromwellians a decade or so later because they were Catholics. Unfortunately, Wentworth's final response in either of these cases is no longer extant, though in Theobald Bourke's 1639 case Wentworth did require Kennedy to make restitution to Bourke.[28]

The last case which we will examine does not directly involve Robert Kennedy but both his brother and his father. It was a case taken by James Walsh (not related to the Carrickmines/Shanganagh Walshes) and his wife Mary in July 1638 against John Kennedy and illustrates the degree of financial distress that both John and Robert Kennedy may have experienced when they lost their chief remembrancer posts. This is also the only document found that mentions their father, also named Robert. James Walsh had married the widow of an attorney who had provided legal services to both John Kennedy and his father in the Court of Common Pleas. She was her late husband's administrator. No date is given, but it would be reasonable to surmise that the service was rendered in either the late 1620s or the early 1630s. The senior Robert had died but had left provision in his will for the attorney, Thomas Cashell, who was to be paid a sum of over £92.[29]

In the documentation there is mention of legal action in very early 1637, yet John Kennedy had persistently refused to engage with James and Mary Walsh over this sum. When Walsh had an attachment made on John, John had met with him and requested mediation. Walsh had agreed, but then John would not again meet with him, which left Walsh in a stalemate. For this reason he had put in a second petition in order to move the case forward. These kinds of shenanigans would suggest a person who is either in dire financial straits or very devious, if not both. John's brother, the younger Robert Kennedy, does not appear to have got involved in this affair.

Another curious detail found in this case is that evidently John was his father's executor, even though Robert was the eldest son. It would confirm an impression that might be inferred from the estate documents, i.e. that Robert Kennedy and his father did not get on. The younger man's conversion to (radical?) Protestantism, his dealings with their wealthy cousins, and his aggressive pursuit of land and wealth to the detriment of his creditors may have offended the older man's sensibilities. The father is not referred to as 'gent' or 'esquire' in this case, so he evidently was not a man of status. The fact that he was alive, perhaps into the early 1630s, yet is only mentioned in passing by someone else in his son's papers is telling. Still, his death would have been part of a difficult decade for Kennedy.

One aspect of Robert Kennedy's operations that might actually have made his financial situation less dire than the above would suggest was his agricultural investment in his Wicklow holdings. The harvest failures in that county through the 1620s had helped in his acquisition of land, but the demand for meat, grain and goods from Irish lands in the 1630s had risen rapidly. This was due to a significant increase in population in both rural and urban areas, driven by relative peace and inward migration. The influx of English (and some Dutch) settlers may also have meant the arrival of energetic workers. They brought with them some of their breeds of cattle, sheep and horses, though these do not appear to have increased yields in any significant way.[30] What did increase yields was their willingness to engage in tillage farming as well as knowing how much could be got from the land.

From the 1641 Depositions we see that Robert Kennedy claimed to be making £400 a year from the sale of agricultural products and rents, with only 25% of this accounted for by the latter. His single most valuable crop was grain and hay, valued at £626 in 1641. He had £600 worth of English cows, which would have contributed to the important live cattle trade to England. Another impressive figure is that he had 3,000 English sheep worth £1,500. Even in November he reported still having £100 worth of wool on his property, most of the summer's shearing having already been sent to market. A further significant item is the presence of English horses. Although only worth £300 in themselves, the offspring of stallions and stud mares would have been of interest to the well-to-do of Dublin, providing high-quality riding and carriage horses. An individual horse only fetched £10, however, not the kind of price to be associated with later stud farms that produced racehorses. Finally, Kennedy was manufacturing bricks. This was fairly common, although for most this activity did not warrant mentioning. The only other landowner who recorded his brick-making in Wicklow was John Pue, though the amount that Kennedy claimed exceeded the other man's by thousands.[31]

A review of the Wicklow entries in the Depositions can put Kennedy's activities into a broader context. Of the Protestant deponents, 42 report losses of £180 or more, twelve of these claiming over £1,000. From these records it becomes possible to see that Protestant farms in County Wicklow were in the business of providing for the needs of Dublin, in terms not only of food but also of other commodities. Milk, butter, cheese, beef, lamb, pork, chicken, turkey, fish, honey, four varieties of grain (wheat, rye, oats and barley), hay, peas, vegetables and malt were being produced in marketable quantities. Moreover, leather, timber, bark (for tanning), wool, charcoal, worked iron goods, fishing nets, and masts and spars for ships could be got from this county.

Compared to his other well-off neighbours (John Hoey in Dunganstown reporting losses of £5,294,[32] William Brabazon, Earl of Meath, £4,257,[33] George Bentley in Milltown £2,700,[34] Henry Harrington in Grangcon £2,535,[35] and his friend John Pue £2,149),[36] Robert Kennedy was running a much larger and more sophisticated agricultural enterprise. None of them came close to his reported loss of £7,000 (which does not include his Dublin and Kildare holdings, for which he posted losses of £380). Kennedy also had such things as a pigeon house, producing a delicacy aimed at the upper end of the market as well as useful fertiliser, and lead pipes and pumps for more efficient access to water. His household goods amounted to nearly

£600, again at least double what these others claimed for this category. His household provisions, at £148, would have needed to include a quantity of wine and spirits, often used in entertaining.

As is ably documented in this work, Robert Kennedy was a man who made everything turn a profit. When possibly accompanying his son Sylvester to Lincoln's Inn in early 1631, he could have researched English farming practices. Sylvester had a personal servant who was English,[37] perhaps someone whom he had employed during his London years. It is therefore not beyond the bounds of possibility that Robert had brought in a farm manager who could have made his holdings produce the above-enumerated results. Alternatively, he could have found him among the numerous Englishmen who had already moved into the county.

It is likely that Robert Kennedy had connections with merchants handling the English trade. Once again his wife's family may have provided him with pertinent contacts. Constance's third brother, Humphrey Sulliard, had married Jane Lee, the daughter of a London man. There is no indication of his business, but he would not have been accepted as a marriage partner unless he was well connected. His being a merchant would be quite plausible. It may also have been the link to Kennedy's making the acquaintance of Thomas Burdett prior to the marriage of their offspring in 1653.

We do know, however, from the Dublin Statute Staple that Kennedy's brother Walter had a business relationship with Alderman Robert Kennedy in 1622, and in 1625 Robert senior had dealings with Philip Conran, who was of a merchant family that had intermarried with Alderman Kennedy's.[38] These families had extensive trading contacts with English ports on the Irish Sea. Even with the feeding of his cattle and stud horses, the large amount of grain that Kennedy was producing would have allowed him to engage in its exportation, as well as having his cattle walked to the Dublin quayside for their onward journey.

The cumulative effect of the corrupt seizure of Irish lands, the result of the English government's determination to 'civilise' Ireland, and the constant denigration of all things Gaelic[39] fed a growing fury within the dispossessed population. For Old English Catholics, it was Parliament's growing crescendo of decidedly anti-Catholic sentiment that collapsed their efforts to be loyal in the face of such hostility.[40] In Wicklow, where Wentworth's 1630s land settlements had opened the gates for settlers, there was intense resentment of the intruders.[41] On

Illus. 15—Portrait of Sir Phelim O'Neill.

22 October 1641, Ulster, led by Sir Phelim O'Neill (Illus. 15), exploded into open rebellion. The uprising in Wicklow started a week later, led by senior O'Byrnes and O'Tooles, though men and women from every level of society participated. In addition, some of the English settlers, confronted with the option of converting or being dispossessed and possibly killed, also joined ranks with local fighters and became 'mass-goers'.

The 1641 Depositions of Wicklow tell us that in the first two weeks settlers up and down the east coast of Wicklow, and somewhat further inland, were attacked, had all their goods taken and were often stripped of their clothing. This last activity served two functions. It gave local Catholics very serviceable material to wear, and it humiliated the people who often had made no secret of their disdain for their uncivilised popish neighbours. In addition, it could be a death sentence, as the weather was particularly cold that year, and some died afterwards of exposure on their trek to friends in Dublin. Others, being forewarned of raiding parties, fled to local castles or tower-houses. These had often been built or taken over precisely in anticipation of resistance and retribution by the previous owners of the land. They were located in Carnew (the southerly most inland area of the county), Arklow, Dunganstown (south of Wicklow), Wicklow, Newrath (just north of Wicklow on the coast), Macreddin (south of Rathdrum), Knockrath (north of Rathdrum, in the mountainous area), Kilruddery (south of Bray) and Powerscourt (in the north-east of the county). None of them, except Wicklow's Black Castle, were able to withstand the attacks or sieges mounted by Gaelic forces. In fact, Capt. Richard Wingfield had abandoned the Powerscourt fortification even before being attacked, and had fled with his men to Dublin. Later testimonies often mention their attackers yelling 'This land is ours!'[42]

In one way the rebellion may have been a relief to Robert Kennedy, as it took people's minds off his skulduggery, but it was also a further serious threat to his financial survival. He perhaps realised that his Ballygarny house would be an object of attack and had absented himself. When insurgent forces arrived at the doorstep of the Ballygarny tower-house in the third week of fighting, only Thomas, in his mid-teens, and his uncle Charles Smith (husband to Robert Kennedy's wife's sister, Margaret) were at home to greet the visitors.

The transcript of the relevant deposition makes very interesting reading, describing as it does a dramatic event in the history of this family. The literal transcription of the record makes it difficult, however, to clearly grasp the import of the text, so I have slightly adapted some of the phrasing to make it more user-friendly. Kennedy's third son, Thomas, had this to say only a few months after the events:

> 'About the [2]3rd or the 24th of last November I saw in front of our towerhouse in Ballygarny about 200 men, ready for battle, about 9 o'clock in the morning. I later learned that they were commanded by Capt. Brian O'Toole, the son of Col. Luke O'Toole, and Capt. Art Brien McCallow O'Byrne, who is from Knockadreet [just east of Roundwood]. The main group of fighters stood about a musket shot's distance from our house.
>
> Brian Tynon from Wicklow town, and Art McGerald O'Byrne of Knockfadda [just north of Knockadreet] approached our house. My Uncle Charles and I were standing on the edge of the motte, looking out over the scene. The two men called out to us, saying they wanted to talk, and that there would be no violence against us. We walked down to them to hear what they had to say. We asked them why they were there. They said that Capt. O'Toole and Capt. O'Byrne wanted to take possession of our residence. Thinking that this was not good news, we asked to speak to these officers personally. …
>
> The next day, Col. O'Toole arrived to the town with more men as well as a small can[n]on. He put this on the hill to the south of our house, and then sent a messenger inviting us to come and speak with him. He guaranteed us safe passage to and from. We went to a house in the town where the colonel explained that he

> had come to fight in the Catholic cause. He said that if I and my father were to become Catholics, he would leave us alone. Otherwise, he would take our house and keep it until he no longer needed it. I said that I wouldn't debate matters of religion; but I and my father would not change our religion. As for this house and the land, there is no one with a better title to them, as my father had paid good money for all of it. He replied, "We have no Court of Chancery here to try the title, but if you yield it not by fair means, let every man stand on his own guard, and we will get it as we can."
>
> Realizing that there was no way we could defend our house against his army, I asked him what terms of surrender he would give us. He said we could depart with our lives, our swords, and some old horses to carry us wherever. We accepted his terms. After we left, they came and occupied the house and took all my father's cattle and corn.'[43]

Just two days later, John Pue (one of Kennedy's trustees and a brother-in-law), in his tower-house at Newrath, was warned by local supporters of the rebellion that if he did not convert to Catholicism he would not escape with his life. He loaded two of his wagons with tubs of butter, 40 quarts of honey, a quantity of cheese and some other provisions, and went up the coast road two miles to Edward Walsh's house at Clonmannan (related to the Shanganagh Walshes and thus to Kennedy), where he spent the night. The next morning he continued his journey to Dublin with four of Ed Walsh's sons, two of his labourers and a Catholic priest. Before they had gone four miles, Capt. Edmond O'Byrne and about 100 men stopped and searched them. They rode on together with the smaller party until they came near Rathdown (just north of what would become Greystones). At that point, a man rode up to the captain and told him that 'Mr Robert Kennedy's Carriages were goeing to Dublin, and that there were stores of muskettes and Pikes sent along with the carriage'. At that point the whole crew sped off in pursuit of Kennedy's wagons.[44] Pue had told these men that he was taking food to his children in Dublin. He was living in one of Kennedy's houses on St Nicholas Street.

Numerous attacks continued for the rest of the month. The Dublin authorities, made desperate by the news that the Wicklow insurgents had set their sights on the city, then sent Col. Charles Coote with a relief party to make his way to Wicklow's Black Castle. He arrived on 29 November and proceeded to indiscriminately slaughter as many men, women and children as he could find in Wicklow town. This significantly broke the momentum of the Wicklow rebellion, and there were only a handful of attacks in the month of December, most of them in the Powerscourt and Bray area, and nearly none after that.

Apart from the obvious loss of land and affront at the religious bigotry and greed that were driving forces in its execution, there was another factor that fuelled the Wicklow rebellion. With the increased agricultural activity in Ireland that characterised the influx of people from Britain, more money was being made by traders, gentry and those in power. This money, now capital, needed avenues of investment. It found them via the institution of the Statute Staple. While not initially set up for this, by the seventeenth century a lot of money was being lent/invested in Ireland through the Staple by those who wanted to increase their wealth. We are fortunate to have the records of the Dublin Staple from 1596 to 1678. Looking at the transactions from 1616 to 1639, we can see that in this period nearly £21,000 had been invested in County Wicklow. Of that sum, O'Byrnes, O'Tooles and O'Cullens had borrowed nearly £14,000. In other words, they were in serious debt. Their land was the collateral on which they had secured their loans. They had nothing more to lose.

Seven months later, Kennedy, accompanied by Col. Crafford and a party of soldiers, went out to County Wicklow to survey the damage. He made a list of the substantial tower-houses he had seen that had been undermined, toppled and burnt in an effort to delay the return of the hated entrepreneurs. These included not only Kennedy's own tower-house and outbuildings but also the tower-houses of Wingfield at Powerscourt, Sir John Hoey (as well as his church) at Dunganstown (south of Wicklow town, just west of the M11), the Earl of Meath at Kilruddery, William Parsons at Milltown (between Glenealy and Rathnew) and John Pue at Newrath.[45]

The blood-letting had been intense; at least 30 people had been killed by the rebels in the space of a month, and after Coote's savaging of Wicklow town there were reprisals against more Protestants. Anyone seen to be cooperating with the Protestant government was likely to be hung forthwith. There is an account by several of the deponents telling of the execution of two English workers, who were also Protestants. Nathaniel Snapp, a servant to Sylvester Kennedy, and John Leeson, a shepherd for the Earl of Meath, had been driving some cattle to Dublin. They happened to be at Ballygarny when the Irish forces occupied the tower-house. After an interview with Col. O'Toole, they were strung up on a tree in the town. Ballygarny residents Anne Roch and David Roch, a ploughman to the Kennedys (and possibly Anne's father-in-law), both assumed that they were killed simply for being English and Protestant,[46] but William Doyle noted that the cattle they were driving had been stolen by Charles Coote on his excursion into Wicklow.[47] This is more likely to have been the reason for their execution.

Once the immediate threat of armed attack and robbery was ended, Robert Kennedy may have tried to rebuild his farm as quickly as his circumstances allowed, but this would not have produced the same income as previously. The general economic decline following the Irish rebellion and during the English civil wars would have considerably reduced the value of goods, and thus his income, from what had previously been a lucrative activity. It is also unclear whether he would have been able to collect rents from his tenants. Most likely it would not have been an option.

Over in England many people had become dissatisfied with the burgeoning power of the king over Parliament that Wentworth had promoted, provoking a rebellious spirit there as well. Thus Charles I found himself under threat on two fronts. He had hoped to settle the 1641 Irish rebellion so that he could use his supporters in Ireland to help him overcome the Parliamentarians, the political manifestation of radical Protestantism. As mentioned above, William Parsons, with radical Protestant leanings, opposed such a settlement in Ireland because it would have disadvantaged his allies in England. Moreover, given his level of greed and anti-Catholic zeal, delaying such a settlement would also have allowed even more land to be confiscated from the rebels. Kennedy had also opposed the Irish Confederacy. Many years later he would write a very sharp letter to his son Richard, making sure that one of his clerks at the Exchequer, John Hope, who had taken up the chief remembrancer's post for the alternate government, was never to be forgiven for his impertinence[48]—this in spite of his previously having been named as one of Kennedy's most trusted clerks in the document outlining Wentworth's bullying.

Estate records from the 1640s and '50s for Robert Kennedy are scarce compared to the abundance of indentures flying to and fro in the 1620s and '30s, so they are no help in our understanding of his activities in these decades. No doubt there were many reasons why he still felt deeply aggrieved by the events of the 1641 rebellion but he had to get on with his life. He could no longer stay in County Wicklow, as his house there had been rendered uninhabitable. He would have retreated to his St Nicholas Street residence for safety's sake and tried to raise some money in whatever way he could. He had submitted a substantial claim for his losses to the government, but it is unlikely that he, or anyone else, ever received compensation. His cash flow would probably have become severely constrained.

One avenue that he pursued for raising money was to take to court anyone he could identify who had stolen property from his estates during the rebellion. He took a case against a Lymerack Nottingham, late of Ballyowen, Co. Dublin (which bordered Kennedy property), for the actions of his servant:

> 'Robert Merryman, servant to [Robt] Kennedy, swears that one Donogh Keagan, one of the said Nottingham's servants, robbed his, Mr Kennedye's, house at Kis-shocke, and still continued in Nottingham's service'.[49]

Lymerack is recorded as having been outlawed during Easter term 1642 for this event, but we have no idea what the outcome was for Kennedy in this case, or how many cases he took. He was certainly not a man to leave any stone unturned.

We can also see that he mortgaged his Kishoge estate to Christopher and Julian Taaffe in June 1643.[50] In August he rented the house north of his own on St Nicholas Street to Dorothy Jones at £10 per year, providing a bit more cash. Further, his loyalty to the English government in Dublin was rewarded with the grant of the office of sheriff for County Wicklow for this same year. In addition, he was made the MP for the borough of Kildare, a post he held for seven years.[51] The money connected with these positions would have provided some relief for his recent losses.

By late 1645, Kennedy's son Richard had finished his training at Lincoln's Inn. After he returned home, he was given the franchise of the city of Dublin, 'by a special grace'.[52] This was a status that his father had never sought. In addition, he was made the MP for Mullingar for the same period. It meant that both he and his father were in the tail-end of the Dublin parliament of 1647. Richard had obviously benefited from the educational and networking opportunities with which his father had provided him. The Dublin government was also looking to bolster the number of their supporters.

Tending towards radical Protestantism, the Kennedys would have welcomed the growing strength of the Parliamentarians under

Cromwell. To lend his support, Richard had become a captain in Kynaston's Parliamentarian regiment (based in Wales) in 1647, staying with it until it was dissolved two years later. Nevertheless, to give some indication of how precarious the politics of the times were, there is a record of Robert Kennedy having been at risk of losing his property owing to Richard's enlistment with the opponents of the king. In the time between Richard's enlistment and the death of the king in January 1649, Robert was declared delinquent—that is, a betrayer of the king. Sir John Dungan had petitioned Ormond for Kennedy's 'delinquent estates in Dublin and Wicklow'.[53]

Yet there had also been a hedging of bets, as his son Thomas evidently had fought with the forces of the Earl of Ormond until his surrender. After the Restoration, Thomas was rewarded with a post in the legal system for his service to the Crown.[54] This specific Earl of Ormond, James Butler (1610–88), was the eleventh earl but also later the first Duke of Ormonde. His political career spanned over 50 years, from 1633 to 1685. One of the few Protestants in his family, he served over a very tumultuous period which included Wentworth's deputyship,

Illus. 16—Portrait of the Earl of Ormond.

the 1641 rebellion and its aftermath, and the land settlement struggle in the early years of the Restoration, much of it as the lord deputy. He spent the Cromwellian decade in exile on the Continent (Illus. 16).

The Parliamentarians continued to gain support and military numbers, and civil war erupted again in England. With no help from Ireland, the Royalists lost ground, and so Charles I lost his head. His son Charles fled to the Continent to bide his time. With his handing over of Dublin to the Parliamentarian forces, Ormond's judgements no longer held sway, and Kennedy's property was no longer under threat. Staying on the right side of whomever was in power was no easy task.

With the triumph of Oliver Cromwell, leader of the Parliamentarians, Ireland again became an object of interest. The Commonwealth needed land to pay its soldiers and exploited what it regarded as the misdeeds of the 1641 rebellion to confiscate whatever land was required. To enforce this option, Cromwell arrived on Irish shores and proceeded to decimate Catholic and Protestant alike, using his presumed godly righteousness to excuse any and all atrocities. He arrived in late 1649 and in under a year had destroyed most centres of resistance.

To further devastate the country, there were several outbreaks of plague. In Dublin in 1651 there was a particularly severe bout, which may have killed up to 40% of the city's population. It struck again in 1652 and 1653.[55] Evidently having no outlying residence to escape the city's toxic environment, Robert Kennedy suffered two painful losses: his eldest son, Sylvester, and his wife, Constance. It is likely that they were buried in the St Nicholas Within graveyard, as that was where his second wife, who died in 1658 after only a few years of marriage, was laid to rest.

The trauma of losing both his eldest son and his wife, after the losses of his coveted post and a productive farm, would have been a difficult blow to bear. Even the most hardened of men would have been severely affected. We have no idea how Robert Kennedy made sense of this turn of events. It is possible, of course, that his first wife had died before 1650, as there is no mention of her death in extant records.

In the Civil Survey of 1654–6 Elizabeth Barlow is recorded as Kennedy's wife (her fourth husband). She brought with her a lease on 33 acres of church land in the parish of Finglas which included a stone house, an old church and a number of farm buildings.[56] In the midst of all this turmoil, Kennedy had managed to arrange marriages for his two younger daughters, which would have cost money. His remarriage may have helped him to cover those costs.

Despite having rental income from his houses on St Nicholas Street, Kennedy found it necessary to mortgage one of these in April 1652.[57] In addition, there was the renegotiation of Mary Crofton Kennedy's marriage portion, as she returned to Temple House in Sligo after Sylvester's death.[58] More money gone! These records give the impression that Kennedy's accumulated wealth was dissipating.

After Cromwell's reconquest of Ireland, completed by 1652, investigations into land ownership got under way. Property owners scrambled to document their rights. Robert Kennedy's 'Clayme before the Commissioners of Revenue Dublin 1653' still survives and attests to his ownership of some land around the southern entrance to the Glen of the Downs, and a number of townlands surrounding Ballygarny.[59] Since Richard had been a Parliamentarian supporter, he was well in with them, and Kennedy was able to keep his land. In fact, Richard was given land in Kilkenny as a reward for his service.[60] Later on, he also purchased 1,500 acres of land from the confiscated Ormond and Sedgrave estates.[61] The Cromwellian years were an especially dark time for Royalist landowners.

In 1656 Robert and John Kennedy attempted to recover one of their posts in the Exchequer which the Cromwellians had removed from them, that of the second chamberlain. They took a case against a John Burniston, who had been appointed by the Protector's patent, on the basis of their letters patent from James I. Interestingly, they won their suit, but Burniston then appealed to the governing council in Ireland and regained his position.[62] The council said that the writ of the king held no authority. It was not until the return of Charles II that Robert regained control of the second chamberlain's post as well as that of chief remembrancer, but it was certainly not for lack of trying.

Radical Protestants combined the usual disdain that Englishmen had for the Irish with religious zeal. The 'papist' Irish were the most ungodly in their eyes, good only for consignment to hell or transplantation to Connaught or the West Indies. They also considered the Established Church to be deluded. The Cromwellian government disestablished this Church but did not punish its members to the same degree as Catholics. Anyone who had been a supporter of the king, however, would have felt the full force of the Cromwellian government's outrage. Apart from a very few, Royalists had no hope of retaining their lands. Survival, expediency and financial stability were the functional values. How each family negotiated these challenges was critical to their continued financial health, if not success. Robert Kennedy's brother Walter, a Catholic, a merchant and a Dublin alderman, chose to resign his membership of that body and moved out of Dublin to his own estate in Clondalkin.[63] Later, when the times had settled, he was able to resurface. He was never again an alderman, but his son Robert was elected to that élite body.

We can see how Robert Kennedy had hitched his wagon to that of William Parsons early on, becoming a Protestant (possibly a radical one) and learning how to serve the major players in the land speculation industry. As this was done primarily through the manipulation of legalities, a career in the courts had been the most useful. His dogged determination to become an owner rather than a tenant fuelled his project. The deft and sly building of alliances was central to this industry and allowed him to accumulate the finances necessary to launch and maintain a family of consequence. That he was able to continue this through the 1650s marks him out as unusually talented in the money game. His clever creativity and ruthless pursuit of property brought him through the loss of a lucrative government post as well as a full-scale rebellion which left many on the wrong side of shifting governments.

Yet the level of trauma which he had sustained throughout his life was quite severe. Given his continued level of functioning, it would be reasonable to surmise that he was a very hardened man, not given to any expression of emotion except, quite possibly, anger.

4
Zenith

Owing to their adroit manoeuvres and networking, the Kennedys had not been unduly threatened by the Parliamentarian storm that left so many others devastated. The next generation, despite the loss of the eldest son, took up the mission of stabilising and expanding the family's wealth. By 1651 Richard had become the heir after Sylvester's death. He had married Ann Barker, daughter of Christopher and Sarah Barker of Buckinghamshire, about 1650.[1] Christopher's grandfather was from Yorkshire and had become a radical Protestant. He had moved to London, keen to publish the Bible in English. According to Janet Kennish:

> 'In 1578 Christopher Barker acquired the title "Printer to Her Majesty the Queen", paying for the privilege which we would call a monopoly, and his son Robert inherited it in 1600. Such titles were bought and sold, inherited and quarrelled over as lucrative trading restrictions; what was at stake was money and power rather than philanthropy or royal goodwill. Robert Barker's greatest achievement was the printing of the King James Bible in 1611, which he claimed to have funded himself to the sum of £3,000.'[2]

This family is quite similar to our Kennedys in a number of ways. The Barkers had come in from the countryside a couple of generations previously, and had done well for themselves as radical Protestants in the capital. Datchet, the site of their country estate, is not far from Windsor Castle.

Richard and Ann Kennedy started their family in 1650 with the birth of a daughter, Constance, followed by the heir, Robert II, in 1651, a second son in 1661, and four more daughters, the youngest being born around 1670.

The question of whether or not the elder Kennedy made his lands at Ballygarny once again a thriving producer of food, animals and other commodities may well have depended on the state of the Irish economy in the 1650s. After the routing of Protestants during the 1641 rebellion and the scourge of Cromwell's murderous, famine-producing drive through Ireland, preparing the way for successive outbreaks of plague in the early 1650s, economic activity in Ireland was much reduced. The loss of population, the decline in food production and the social upheaval of a Cromwellian government in Dublin would have made it difficult for people to produce the same level of surplus or to have a market for it.

Trade records do show, however, that barrelled beef and dairy products like butter and cheese continued to be exported.[3] Whether Newcastle barony could support dairying to the same degree as Munster is unclear, but finding workers and a manager to drive Kennedy's farm yields is more likely to have been the crucial factor. The only possible exception to this otherwise subdued picture may have been the development of mills on what would become manor property.

There are references to a mill on the Cooladoyle stream, around which there was a hamlet, as early as 1624.[4] It is difficult to know how long it had been there. There is one 1636 indenture which dictates that the tenant must grind his corn at the mill of Robert Kennedy in Ballygarny, which shows the continuance of this same mill.[5] (There are no longer even the ruins of a mill at this location.) This stream, currently known as the Altidore River, runs along the southern boundary of the demesne and then through Kilmacullagh, which is the land to the east of Newtownmountkennedy's main street. There are still the ruins of two mills on it. The older of these would have been a grain mill and is located off the Kilcoole road, just into the townland of Killadreenan. The other is evidently a more recent building (though it may have been built over an older mill). In a 1672 indenture there is a reference to the 'new mill'.[6] Shortly after this there start to be references in indentures requiring that tenants' homespun and woven cloth be tucked (or fulled) at the manor mill.[7] These mills would have been a source of income for the manor, but as there is no reference to income from a mill in 1641, or later, it is impossible to know how much they contributed to Kennedy's income.

In the 1650s Richard had lands in counties Tipperary and Kilkenny, previously part of the Ormond estate, but there is likewise no indication that these made any significant financial contribution. In any event, they were given back to Ormond at the Restoration, along with land associated with John Sedgrave.[8]

It is more likely, therefore, that Robert Kennedy and his sons, and perhaps his brother John and his sons, concentrated on a legal practice to keep themselves afloat in the 1650s. Richard had served as counsel for Phelim O'Neill at his trial in 1652 for his involvement in the Irish Confederacy.[9] His being chosen for this role would indicate that his profile was high in Dublin. Representing someone with a Gaelic surname may also have given the impression of impartiality. Although the case was lost, it would have brought him to further prominence in the legal world, and he was admitted to the King's Inns in 1656, along with his brother Thomas, evidence of their continued prestige during the Interregnum.[10]

Remarkably, there survives the transcript of one of Richard's legal opinions, in which he comports himself well. A number of judges delivered opinions before His Grace the Lord Chancellor of Ireland in the case between John St Leger Esq., plaintiff, and John Barrett Esq., defendant. This transcription was taken by the Register of the High Court of Chancery in 1678/9.[11] The fact that Richard was asked to comment in the Chancery would indicate that, as a judge, his legal expertise continued to be held in esteem.

The family's combined resources allowed Robert Kennedy to pay off his mortgaged house on St Nicholas Street in 1654,[12] but when his daughter Bridget, widowed by the death of Michael Doyne, married Philip Harris[13] in 1658, all he could offer was an IOU for £600. (It would not be fully paid until the late 1690s.[14]) Bridget's son, Robert Doyne, later trained in law, however, and would go on to become a chief justice first of the Court of the Exchequer and later of the Common Pleas. Did his grandfather have a hand in this?

The Kennedys were of a decidedly conservative bent, and with the demise of the Cromwellian government Richard's position started to shift to a Royalist one. In 1659 Richard, in his mid-30s, was one of the members for County Wicklow at the Irish Convention, a group of eminent men and landowners who assembled to discuss how Cromwellian rule was to be replaced. He went on to be one of the commissioners who, at the behest of the provisional Irish government, went to London in 1660 to petition for the return of Charles II.[15] Obviously, he had been quite adept at impressing the power brokers in Ireland, initially the Parliamentarians and later the Royalists.

Nevertheless, his Parliamentarian background had not been forgotten: despite acting on behalf of the English government in Ireland, he was one of a group of 78 officers in Ireland who were given a general pardon.[16] He had also been nominated for the post of recorder for the Dublin city government but was not successful.[17] No reason has come down to us for his lack of success in this instance, but no doubt competition for the post was intense.

Aidan Clarke has pointed out that Richard was 'part of the marital web of the Dublin office holders'.[18] This élite network, firmly anchored by their marriage to the daughters of William Parsons, included such luminaries as Paul Davis, William Usher, James Barry, John Hoey and Arthur Hill. Richard's older brother's widow had gone on to marry Paul Davis (after his previous wife had died). It is interesting that this web had continued despite the death of Parsons in 1650. Relatedness by marriage—and, down the line, by blood—wove a strong net.

F.E. Ball, working in the early twentieth century, carried out a lot of research on Richard and had access to documents no longer extant. He notes that

> 'Towards the Restoration, both Kennedy and his father rendered important services, which received subsequently a reward in places and honours. In addition to his seat in the Exchequer [as the second Baron of the Court], Kennedy was given the office of attorney of the Court of Wards, and received from the hands of the King the honour of knighthood, while his father was restored to the office of chief remembrancer, of which he had been deprived by the Parliament [*sic*], and was granted a baronetcy.'[19]

Ball goes on to note that the Court of Wards was dissolved shortly after his appointment, so that Richard lost emoluments of £1,000 per year. He was able to get a rise of £100 for his Exchequer post but was still financially diminished. Perhaps to improve his income he undertook the assizes in Ulster, where he was known for suppressing Dissenters and overseeing deportations to Jamaica.[20] Gilbert mentions grants to Richard of confiscated lands, with nearly 4,600 acres in Carlow, 800 in Kilkenny and 262 in Wicklow that had been part of these honours.[21] It would appear that the lands in Carlow and Kilkenny were sold, as they are never mentioned in the estate papers or in any other listing of townlands in the estate. This would have provided Richard with a significant windfall.

The Kennedys' Ballygarny residence had been rehabilitated at some point. Whether this was by the rebuilding of the tower-house or the construction of a more fashionable seventeenth-century abode is impossible to say, though the latter is much more probable. In 1660 Robert had been granted the right to hold a Thursday market and two two-day fairs on his estate.[22] These would have added to the estate's income.

Robert Kennedy continued to lease more of his Dublin property. He also required that ash trees be planted on his properties to increase their value.[23] He knew how to make everything turn a profit. He was also an obsessive record-keeper—a very important practice in the tumultuous seventeenth century. In 1662 Jonathan Edwards, the minister of St Nicholas's Church, on behalf of the Vicars Choral of St Patrick's, took a case against Robert for non-payment of rents due to the Vicars for the use of their land under some of his St Nicholas Street houses. Robert was able to produce receipts (still extant) from 1630 for one of these houses but had to pay £25 for arrears on another.[24] Meanwhile, Richard, as happens with judges, found gifts coming his way. Sir Maurice Eustace, then lord chancellor of Ireland, left him £20 in his will for a ring.[25]

In early 1662 Richard attended the House of Lords in London, apparently as an adviser to the House. Expense accounts were not part of the picture in those days, however, so such a trip would have incurred significant costs. He went there again in 1664 as an agent for the city government, looking to have Dublin's privileges restored. In recognition of his efforts he was given an engraved plate worth £50.[26] This still did not pay the bills.

Richard had been groomed by his father for a rise in status, and owing to fortuitous historical circumstances he was now an Exchequer judge before he was 40 years old. The visit of the Duke of Ormond to the Kennedys' house in Wicklow in 1662 was a notable achievement on their part, as Ormond was the most powerful and socially important man in Ireland at that time.[27] It is likely that he was Richard's patron politically and was probably the one to see to it that Richard was given an annual pension of £800 in October of that year.[28] This would cover some bills. Nevertheless, when Richard applied for the post of Chief Justice of Common Pleas three years later, he was passed over for an Englishman, Edward Smyth, despite having bought the reversion for the post.[29]

Why did Richard not get that post? Evidently the power of a

reversion had deteriorated considerably. There has been some suggestion that Richard's severity as an assize judge in Ulster had put him into Ormond's bad graces, but no evidence is given for that assertion.[30] Once again, it is F.E. Ball who provides the explanation for the appointment. English judges were considered superior to Irish ones;[31] even before the previous Chief Justice Donnellan died, the Earl of Clarendon had been negotiating with another English judge, who ultimately decided not to take the post. The Earl of Ossory, Ormond's son, had recommended Edward Smyth,[32] and Ormond went along with that. Richard Kennedy was never in the running. It had very little to do with what he had or had not done. He simply had not distinguished himself as a judge in the way that Smyth had, nor was he English.[33]

Looking more closely at the man who did get the appointment, Edward Smyth, we can see that he was very competent and experienced. He had worked at the Bar in England, as well as having served as a judge in the Court of Claims for the Restoration land settlement. In this capacity he had impressed Ormond with his rulings, and this would appear to be the reason why he was awarded the Common Pleas post.

In hindsight, it can be seen that this was a pivotal moment in the fortunes of the Kennedys. Through missing out on the more prestigious post, Richard's government networking circle had been greatly reduced. His son had only a second chamberlain's post at the Exchequer, and no way of negotiating anything more. If English history had been less fraught in the last two decades of the seventeenth century, the family might have been able to maintain their manor and go on for generations, but this was not to be.

Landownership in Ireland in the decade of the 1660s was in a state of chaos. Many owners had been dispossessed for their reputed activities during the 1641 rebellion, while others had been given this same land for their service in the Parliamentarian army or for funding that side in the war. A court was commenced to try to administer justice for the many caught up in this mess. During the very contentious Restoration land settlement process, petitions from dispossessed landowners were put before the Court of Claims.[34]

During this process, Robert Kennedy responded forcefully to a threat to his great-grandson, John Walsh of Shanganagh, who was in danger of being dispossessed of his lands. (John's grandfather, John, had married Robert's daughter Mary.) 'Robert acted as guardian to his grandson [*sic*], a minor whose father was dead, and presented the claim to the court. The decree was issued in Kennedy's name with John declared an innocent Protestant.'[35] Despite his advanced age, Robert was still able to exercise influence in the newly restored royal government, though most likely with the significant help of his son Richard.

It is not clear whether 'innocent Protestant' refers only to Robert or to both of them. John was only six or seven years old, so his denominational adherence could have been asserted for a practical reason. It is known, however, that John's sons were Catholics.[36] By this time, even Robert's brother Walter had succumbed to the necessity of adopting Protestantism if he were to keep even a tenth of the property left to him.[37] Their brother John and his descendants, however, managed to remain Catholics on their lands in Longford into the eighteenth century,[38] but then that family evidently moved to France.[39]

Finally, on 28 September 1664, King Charles II enacted letters under the Great Seal which made the landholdings of Robert Kennedy into a manor to be known as Mount Kennedy.

> 'Kennedy shall have power to set aside 3,000 acres for demesne lands and may aliene [lease] in fee or for lives such part as he shall think fit, and shall hold of us and our heirs … "in free and common socage or by suit of court … [and] by any other lawful reservations". He shall have a court leet and view of frankpledge, may impark 500 acres, or more or less, for deer and shall have other manorial rights … and may hold a Court of Record within the manor of Mount Kennedy by himself or his seneschal with jurisdiction of pleas in personal actions up to £4.'[40]

The document declaring Robert's lands a manor lists twenty townlands comprising nearly 6,500 modern acres.[41] These can be seen in Illus. 11 in the darker shading. Not named are a number of townlands that he had previously been said to own. These are noted on the map by their names being in bold italics.[42] Just a month later, the anticipated completion of his honours came when a baronetcy was bestowed on him. This would have cost him a sizeable sum of money; from the Crown's point of view, such titles were a good source of revenue.

What is not mentioned in the establishment of his manor is that Robert, and later Richard, had been a property developer on St Nicholas Street, as well as amassing lands in Wicklow. It is not initially obvious from the scattering of indentures referring to houses on this street that Robert not only bought up a number of houses but also built

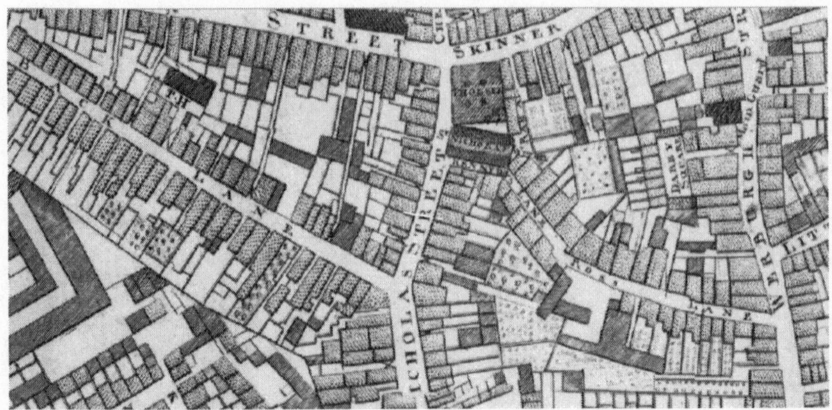

Illus. 17—Detail from Rocque's 1756 Dublin map (from Colm Lennon, *Irish Historic Towns Atlas No. 19: Dublin, Part II, to 1756* (Dublin, 2008); used with permission).

some, if not all, of them, after quite possibly having torn down already existing structures (if Speed's map is to be believed).

An eighteenth-century account of Dublin's history noted that up until the reign of Elizabeth I most of the buildings in Dublin were of mud and wattle, and thatched (as they had been in the time of the Vikings). It was only in the mid-sixteenth century that what are known as cagework buildings, roofed with slates,[43] began to be built (see Illus. 9). Large beams were used to build a framework to support the building, the 'cage', and then the spaces were filled in with plaster. The buildings that Kennedy took down were probably of mud and wattle construction.

This can be most clearly seen with regard to Jenefields Inns. The footprint of the property on which at some point a mansion was built matches that of this medieval tower and hall (which Robert would have demolished for their building materials) and large garden.[44] Although the plot involved did not front onto St Nicholas Street, it did have an access lane which was called Kennedys Lane by the early seventeenth century (Illus. 17). What seems likely is that Robert tore down some of the older houses between the street and the garden. This would have allowed him to build the much larger house, probably of brick, with an imposing presence. An attractive front lawn would have set it off nicely (a figure of 28ft to the street is mentioned).

In the late 1670s this house was leased to a man who turned it into a tavern, calling it The Golden Fleece, and then built himself a residence behind the tavern, with still enough space for a garden behind that again.[45] Robert Kennedy was also housing some of his extended family in his St Nicholas Street holdings. Philip Harris, a son-in-law married to Robert's daughter Bridget, was said to be occupying the rear of one house, while Robert Pue, most likely a son of John Pue senior, occupied the front.[46] In this way, the Kennedys would have dramatically transformed the east side of St Nicholas Street over the course of the seventeenth century.

One could imagine that the now Sir Robert Kennedy was immensely pleased with these developments. He was an elderly man at this point (probably very close to 80), and in fact he only lived for another four years. By the yardstick of his times, he had done very well for himself. He had taken the route of working in the courts rather than being a merchant like his brother Walter and other branches of the family. While Walter had been granted the freedom of the City of Dublin and had been made an alderman,[47] he does not appear to have been as wealthy as Robert, nor was he able to reach the distinction of a title. Partly this would have been due to his having remained a Catholic for most of his life, converting only to save his lands after the Restoration. Robert had sought out service with one of the most cunning wheeler-dealers of his time (Parsons) and had transformed himself into a New English Protestant. His son was an Exchequer judge, with two sons, and he could reasonably have expected that his line would continue to hold power and wealth well into the future.

While this social advancement was in train, Richard's daughters were coming of marriageable age. In September 1667 Richard entered into Articles of Agreement with John Parry, then dean of Christ Church,[48] which office came with a handsome remuneration of £660.[49] Parry also owned the lease of houses and shops on College Green, including Chichester House, later to be called Parliament House. His father, of Welsh birth, had been the bishop of Killaloe. John had been educated at Trinity College Dublin but then went on to Oxford after 1649, where he established himself as a writer of pious reflections and scholarly works. Shortly after the Restoration he had become chaplain to Ormond. He did not accompany the duke on his return to Ireland but stayed in England until 1664. When he did return, he went first to Cork before being appointed the dean of Christ Church in 1666. In a sermon there he likened Ormond to an Old Testament hero, and was made the bishop of Ossory the following year.[50]

Richard Kennedy, perhaps using his own Ormond connection, must have moved fairly quickly to secure the eligible bachelor for his eldest daughter.[51] The marriage portion was very large—£1,000—though this was at least partly funded by Sir Maurice Eustace.[52] Later Parry would have had not only the Christ Church salary but also £400 from the bishop's annual income at Ossory,[53] making life very comfortable for the couple. Parry was at least seventeen years older than Constance, however, and after eight years of marriage he provided for her in the event of his death in a March 1675/6 set of legal documents.[54] He died in December 1677,[55] evidently childless. By 1679 Constance had gone on to marry Col. John Seymour, whose older brother was Speaker of the British House of Commons.[56]

Clergy, and especially those with connections that would lead them to bishoprics, were attractive marriage partners owing to the considerable patronage they had at their disposal. As an assize judge in Ulster, Richard would have been aware that the local bishop often sat in the court with him or provided room, board and entertainment at his palace for the visiting judge. Bishops could give appointments to clergymen, and also license curates, physicians, church courts and other local administrators.[57]

It should come as no surprise, therefore, that Richard Kennedy's match for his next daughter was to another well-educated former chaplain to Ormond, Welshman Edward Jones. Jones was apparently still the headmaster of the boys' grammar school in Kilkenny (a post given to him by Ormond in 1670 on his arrival in Ireland) when he married Elizabeth around 1679. In 1683 he was made bishop of Cloyne, Co. Cork.[58] Elizabeth, being Richard's third daughter, only received a marriage portion of £800. Cloyne was the bishopric of the least value in all Ireland, being only somewhat over £400,[59] but it provided the connection for the marriages of two more Kennedy sisters.

Within twelve months of Elizabeth's marriage, Richard's second daughter Sarah was wedded to Gilbert Heathcote, a curate at Youghal. He had previously taken a Master's at Christ's College, Cambridge. His father had been a captain in a Parliamentarian regiment in Ireland in 1658, and may have been known to Richard through his Parliamentarian connections. Being on a more modest income, her £1,000 marriage portion would have been much appreciated by the couple.[60] In 1685, doubtless owing in part to Kennedy family connections, Heathcote was made chancellor of Cloyne. He remained there until 1693, when it is said that he was deprived for Nonconformity.[61] At that time the couple moved to Wicklow and lived at Mount Kennedy.

The youngest of Richard Kennedy's daughters, Bridget (not to be confused with her aunt of the same name), whose marriage portion was only £600, was married to Edward Jones's younger brother, Matthew, who had come over to Ireland with Edward. He had entered Trinity College Dublin in 1673 and was ordained in 1680 at Kilkenny. It seems likely that they married around 1684, when he was preceptor of Cloyne; he was given the prebendary of Donoughmore in 1687.[62] The couple, who had six children, are both buried at Inniscarra parish, west of Cork city.

Richard's fourth daughter, Ann, with a marriage portion of £800,[63] was married to George Burdett, from the same place in County Carlow as the husband of Richard's aunt, Catherine Kennedy Burdett. Evidently connections between the two families had not only remained intact but also recommended a further liaison! According to Betham's *Pedigrees,* George was the son of Thomas and Catherine.[64] A dispensation may have been secured for the marriage of these first cousins but it was not legally required at the time. George and Ann only had one child, Catherine, who married a Revd Daniel Savile. There is a surviving family tree that gives us information about further offspring; it was composed by Catherine's descendants in 1826.[65]

Although Richard had five daughters, the level of society into which he was able to marry them (apart from Constance) was not one that would provide useful connections for political advancement. His father had done well in securing the Crofton marriage for his eldest son. This father-in-law was above Robert at the Exchequer, and if tragedy had not overtaken Sylvester the family's fortunes might have continued to rise. John Parry had political connections via Ormond, but Ormond was well advanced in years, and by the time he died the political landscape in Ireland was much changed. Again, the birth of a child, especially a son, would have kept the Kennedys connected to the Parrys, a family of note, but this did not happen.

A month after arranging Constance's marriage in 1667, Richard bought over 6,500 acres (modern) of land in Newcastle Barony for £1,400 from Sir John Borlase, who had been granted it by the king. It included sixteen townlands[66] and more or less doubled the size of the Kennedy holdings. The sale of lands in Kildare and Carlow would have facilitated this purchase. The William Kennedy who is one of the witnesses to this transaction must be Richard's cousin, a son of either Walter or John, as his own son William was only five or six years old at this time. All these townlands are in the lighter shading in Illus. 11, including others named below.

No doubt Richard's father would have been impressed by his son's expansion of their estate. Richard was obviously spending a lot of money, between marriage portions and land acquisition, but then Robert had done the same. He was lucky to see it happen; just a few months later, in March 1668, he passed away, in his early 80s. According to his funeral entry, he is 'buried in the country'. The Newcastle parish records tell us that he was buried in the chancel of the medieval Delgany church on 18 March.[67] There would have been a vault for the family, with a monument over it, but there is nothing to be seen in the chancel of the old church today except a flat patch of ivy.

Sir Richard continued to make use of his contacts in the army to scoop up more land from soldiers who had been given it as payment for their services. Between 1669 and 1672 he obtained an additional 1,770 acres[68] from Col. Heyward St Ledger and others for the minimal sum of £64. These lands were south and west of his main holdings. By this time his son, Robert II, had also started working as the second chamberlain of the Exchequer.[69] His grandfather had continued to hold the assignment of this post and had passed it on for his descendants to start out as he had.

Just two years after his father died, it is said that Sir Richard built a 'large mansion house' on Mount Kennedy, which was later burned in the Williamite wars.[70] This would have required a significant financial outlay. He had also just spent over £1,400 on land acquisition and £4,200 on marriage portions. The restoration of the monarchy had also restored the penchant for lavish spending by the rich and famous, who were living beyond their means despite their wealth. With his significant loss of income after the demise of the Court of Wards, questions about Richard's financial health start to niggle, even with the windfall from the sale of granted lands.

Evidence of financial strain can be deduced from a number of events. In 1675, when Sir Richard's son, Robert II, was ready to enter Lincoln's Inn, £100 had to be borrowed, with surety provided by his mother.[71] In March 1675/6, transactions were set up between Richard and John Parry, now bishop of Ossory, to cover the unpaid portion of Constance's dowry, again indicating an obligation not met.[72] In 1679 Richard conveyed his estate to a trust composed of the archbishop of Armagh, the archbishop of Dublin, Sir Maurice Eustace (privy councillor), Henry Hene (a baron of the Exchequer), Sir William Domville (attorney-general), Sir John Temple (solicitor-general), Edward Jones (then dean of Lismore), Walter Walsh, gent (Richard's nephew), and George Kennedy, merchant (a cousin, son of John

Kennedy, Richard's uncle).[73] As previously mentioned, a trust was a way to safeguard's one's estate before and after death, to protect it from creditors and keep it in the family. Lastly, the large amount of money and land extracted from the Howards as a dowry when Robert II was to wed Frances, daughter of Dr Ralph Howard, in 1682 would again make one wonder about the Kennedy finances.[74]

In August 1672, Sir Richard protested his financial straits by petitioning for further remuneration from the Crown, listing his gradual loss of government income, including a reduction of his judge's salary and perquisites. He suggested how this might be remedied:

> 'In 1660 his Majesty promised to be further favourable to [me], yet [my] condition is much harder now than then as aforesaid, and therefore praying that his Majesty will appoint [me] one of the Commissioners of Appeals with a salary, or continue to [me] the said salary of £120 for the attorneyship of the Court of Wards.'[75]

The latter would have meant paying him for doing nothing. None of this came to pass.

Sir Richard appears not to have been fond of consistency. After complaining of penury, we see that he built yet another house on St Nicholas Street, this one of brick with piped water.[76] Of course, he was able to rent it for what would have been a large sum of money. It takes money to make money after all. Just a year and a half prior to this, he had also used a front man to purchase another house on the street, which he then transferred into his name in early 1680.[77] This would account for the seven houses that he mentioned as being in his ownership on St Nicholas Street in 1679.[78]

Estate business also continued apace through the 1670s. It is probable that most of the documents of this time have been lost, as there are less than half a dozen in the file. (Another possibility is that a later request for deeds by the husband of the then heir was granted in part.) Transactions for two houses on St Nicholas Street, one in Newtownmountkennedy, one for Kilpedder townland and one for Callowhill/Kilday townlands are all that remain. Part of the loss of documentation may also be connected to the fact that Sir Richard was becoming senile.

The lease relating to Newtownmountkennedy is of note because it is the first one extant that is dated after the creation of the manor. It was made to Henry Livesly, a 'cordwinder' (shoemaker), on 1 April 1672.[79] This is the first time we see the full name 'Newtownmount-kennedy' used in an estate document.[80] In addition, the house was rented to a settler as opposed to a local person from Wicklow. Interestingly, the Down Survey lists William Parsons as the owner of Newtown in 1671. It is unclear how this could have been the case. Sir William Parsons had died in 1650, so this William Parsons would have been his grandson. It could be that the final transfer from the trust, headed by Sir William and inherited by the younger man, only happened in 1672, allowing the lease to be part of the estate's papers, but other leases on townlands held in trust under Sir William are present in the earlier documentation. It is more likely, then, that Parsons had owned Newtown, and it only became part of the estate's business after Sir Richard bought the townland. In any case, the previous most recent extant transaction in the Kennedys' Wicklow holdings before 1672 had been in 1639, evidencing the level of upheaval and disorganisation that had characterised the area for those decades.

At the same time as the trust document was drawn up, Sir Richard had also made his last will and testament. In this he outlined what his wife was to receive—all his goods and chattels as well as the plate, hangings, brass and pewter in their St Nicholas Street dwelling, all the goods in their County Dublin Ballydowd property, and her choice of their coaches along with two of the coach horses. These would revert to their son Robert II on her death. This list gives us some insight into the level of comfort in which they were living.[81] From the trust document we learn that William was to be given £50 a year until he turned 30 years old, or until he took up the office of second chamberlain of the Exchequer or came into the estate of his uncle Thomas (who had no children).

This revelation that Thomas and his wife had been childless, as had been Sylvester and his wife, may highlight one of the hidden dangers of life in Dublin, which actually has persisted into the modern period—lead poisoning. In the medieval period, Dublin got its water from upstream on the Dodder River. It was diverted and ran as a stream before being transported in a wooden trough for its onward journey to the city. Once in the city, however, it was put into lead pipes, these being less prone to degradation than other types of metal.[82] A well-known consequence of exposure to lead is infertility, in both men and women. If both Sylvester and Thomas had had children, this would have significantly increased the family's chances of survival in the coming decades.

Indeed, these pipes may also have played a part in the fact that although Alderman Robert Kennedy had seven sons none of them had children either. Their house was on Back Lane, which was the location of one of the earlier feed pipes in the city. Even though most people drank ale instead of water, the water used for the ale came though the lead pipe as well. Most houses made their own ale. This could be considered another trauma arising from living in the city, but one that was not identified until much later.

Sadly, Sir Richard's senility was officially confirmed in an August 1681 document.[83] Puzzlingly, some sources state that Sir Richard died in this year. This is evidently based on the record of his burial in the St Nicholas Within register on 11 August.[84] There is a note indicating that this information came from a 'Mr Martin'. The estate records, however, continue to state that Robert II is acting for his father until early in 1685, when Richard is said to be deceased. Perhaps owing to his becoming officially senile in 1681, someone thought that his relative absence in Dublin indicated his death.

On 25 October 1682 the Kennedys celebrated the next generation's commitment to the family's continuance—the marriage of Robert II and Frances Howard. Her father owned Shelton, near Arklow (later to be known as Shelton Abbey). To give some idea of how young a woman could be when she married, the *DIB* tells us that Ralph Howard had married Catherine Sotheby in 1668, which means that Frances was at most fourteen years old on her wedding day.[85]

Ralph Howard was also a doctor, a professor of medicine at Trinity College, and a founding member and first president of the College of Physicians. He had come into his property by marrying the only child of Robert Hassells, the original settler of Shelton and his mother's first cousin. As mentioned previously, if this Kennedy/Howard marriage had not taken place our ability to tell this story would be seriously hampered. It was the Howard family that would continue on for centuries, and with them would go the Kennedy papers.

Robert II drove a hard bargain with Ralph, demanding a marriage portion of £2,200. In exchange for this he would set up a trust into which County Wicklow land worth £300 per annum would be put.[86] In addition, the two lots of land owned by Robert Hassells in County Wexford, in the baronies of Gorey and Bargy, would also be held for the sole use of Robert II and Frances. Lastly, if Robert Hassells or his wife would have more than £1,000 when they died, the excess would also go to Robert II and his wife.[87] The Kennedys were a much more important family than the Howards at that point, and the latter were going to have to pay to move up in the world. It was reasonably anticipated that they would benefit through their new in-laws, and therefore that their other children would marry 'up' as well, helped out by their Kennedy connection.

Perhaps because everyone's finances were so encumbered by debt, the legal documents surrounding the joining of these two families were very professionally executed. There were a number of them, each addressing a specific aspect of the arrangements between the two families.[88] Despite this difficulty, Robert II evidently was genuinely devoted to Frances and took steps to safeguard her family. Her father's feelings about all of this are less in evidence at this point.

The first child of this marriage, Richard II, was born on 11 August 1684.[89] It would appear that he was baptised in the Kennedys' Dublin parish, indicating that this very social event was saved for the capital's social circle. Once again, however, the date given in the St Nicholas parish register is four years off the mark, courtesy of 'Mr Martin'.

The 1660s and '70s had indeed been prosperous decades for the Kennedys of Mount Kennedy. Their continued astute choices on who to back in the leadership of Ireland and England, and their flexibility in terms of religious expression, had allowed them to weather political storms that defeated many of their countrymen. They were prominent as a legal family, and continued to produce heirs as needed. Yet Richard's failure to secure a chief justiceship may indicate that the family's status had started to slip.

5

Things Fall Apart

The 1680s proved to be the undoing of the Kennedys of Mount Kennedy. We will explore the factors that brought about their decline, comprising both bad luck and larger forces beyond their control. With the failure of the 1641 rebellion, Cromwell's crushing of all resistance and the influx of yet more English settlers, the situation in Ireland was felt to be more stable, thus requiring less attention in terms of hands-on control. Practically speaking, this meant that the late seventeenth century saw more and more of the governing power shifting from Dublin to London.[1] The import of this for our Kennedys was that, as a middle-ranking family who needed someone of greater influence than themselves to maintain their importance, there were fewer influencers with whom they could align themselves. Without some presence at the royal court, opportunities for appointments and land grants could not be had. Richard's network had declined precipitously after he failed to win the post of a chief justice, significantly threatening the family's economic security.

In the early seventeenth century, the senior Kennedy had been able to tap into a network of radically inclined Protestants who were very powerful, but with the death of Cromwell, the general disillusionment with radical Protestantism and the resurgence of the Established Church under the restored Crown this path to influence was no longer available. Moreover, Richard's son, Robert II, does not appear to have had the level of ambition that had been required of his father and grandfather to prosper politically and financially. As often happens in families where earlier generations have worked hard to get ahead, later generations tend to take their wealth for granted and be less driven.

This could be where trauma, or the lack of it, played a part. Robert II was born in 1651 into an established family of significant status. True, times were brutal in Ireland, as Cromwell wreaked havoc and mayhem, but a five-year-old in such a family would have been well protected. His father had been a Cromwellian officer, and it is unlikely that there was much sense of alarm in Robert II's environment. The death of his mother and brother would have been upsetting for Richard, but not occasions of threat to the family's security. If anything, it improved their status, as Richard then became the new heir. He would have prioritised keeping up with his perceived peers, which required the expenditure of large sums of money.[2] Robert II's comfortable family situation would have engendered an expectation that it would always be thus.

Sir Richard Kennedy died in January 1684/5. This meant the loss of whatever income he had still been receiving, most notably his pension of £800 per year. The income of a second chamberlain was woefully inadequate to the lifestyle of a baronet. From here on out, the estate would have to pay its own way. Given its size, over 13,000 acres, it should have been producing a good income.

The earliest extant financial account of any sort for the estate is a brief abstract dated from Lady Day (25 March) 1686 to the same for 1693, indicating from whom income was received and to whom it was going.[3] The estate manager during this period, and the compiler of this account, was George Antrobus, who was responsible for collecting the rents and running the farm. It is not clear whether the sums involved are for one year or all seven. The total income is given as just over £5,151. If this is divided by seven, it would give an average yearly income of about £735, which is roughly the same as that given for later individual years. It could be surmised that the initial years were noticeably higher, owing to the significant drop in rents after 1690. Indeed, out of the above total income, 46% was said to be in arrears.

These accounts are further perplexing because income is tallied not only for those renting houses in Newtownmountkennedy or townlands but also for those paying only several pounds, obviously for other reasons. All the payees are down the left-hand side of the sheets, with those receiving the money across the top of the columns. Antrobus is shown to be receiving 33% of all the expected income (60% of the actual income), but a quick check of the written total for the income on the first page shows that it is short by nearly £90. Even with accounts being done, it was all too easy for the manager to pocket a significant amount of the income. Later, when he learned that he was suspected of embezzlement, he replied that he had none of the estate money, something contradicted by his own record.[4]

There is not enough documentation on Sir Robert II to provide any indication of how he interacted with those around him. Was he spending most of his time in Dublin, working in the Exchequer, or did he deputise his post and spend most of his time socialising? Was he keeping an eye on the estate? A later letter only tells us that he was devoted to his mother and very religious.[5] The senior Robert had been fired both by his awareness of the amount of wealth and power to be had and by a visceral sense of danger if he did not rise in social status. These factors would have driven his ambition. His sons would have been involved in the business affairs of the family at an early age to impress the work ethic upon them, but the younger Robert had not had the benefit of these influences. Family tradition sent him to the best schools, and living in a big house was all that he knew.

On the level of the larger picture, events in England once again impinged on its neighbour, specifically the monarchy and matters of religion. It was rumoured that the aging King Charles II's younger brother was a Catholic. Since Charles had no sons, his brother James would inherit the throne. There had been a number of conspiracy theories circulating in London in the late 1670s and early 1680s, painting dire pictures of the threat of a Catholic resurgence. The general English populace lived in dread of a Catholic king.

In the month following Sir Richard's death King Charles II died. James II ascended the throne in April, and as events unfolded it became obvious that he was going to shake up the Irish government in terms of Catholics and Protestants, despite his earlier indications that he would not. Still, with the birth of an heir, Richard II, the previous August, Robert II may have hoped that he could ride out the storm by staying in place. He continued with family transactions set in motion by the deaths of his father and his uncle Thomas (Thomas died in April 1684 and was buried in the St Nicholas Within graveyard[6]).

On 1 April 1685, Sir Robert II enacted an indenture in which he passed on to his brother William, then around 24 years old, property that their father had wanted him to have.[7] William had been studying at Lincoln's Inn since 1681 but doubtless made the occasional trip home to Dublin. The major portion of the bequest was a lot of ten houses on Kennedy's Lane. This lane started at St Nicholas Street and ran eastwards along the southern side of St Nicholas's Church; it was originally the access lane for Jenefields Inns. Apart from a mention in an indenture in 1682 concerning Sir Richard's previous residence on St Nicholas Street, whose northern boundary consisted of the backs of these houses, there is no previous mention of them in the extant estate papers.

Gilbert, in his history of Dublin, stated that Kennedys had built those houses in the reign of James I.[8] Since he only mentions the chief remembrancer, others have assumed that he was the builder, but *that* Robert didn't have the money for that level of construction at that time. Moreover, their invisibility in the estate papers, despite numerous mentions of the building of the St Nicholas Street houses, would suggest that they were built by Alderman Robert Kennedy. This conclusion was also reached by the *Irish Builder* in the late nineteenth century.[9] The houses would have been taken in the capture of the alderman's property via the Court of Wards. The only other property to come into William's ownership was a twenty-acre plot in Donaghmore, Co. Kildare, which is just east of Maynooth on the Dublin road.[10]

Perplexingly, on 6 April William signed a memorandum in which he acquiesced to his loss of the post of the second chamberlain of the Exchequer, which his brother had sold to someone else. As he physically held the deed for this office, he promised to hand it over. His sister Ann, his brother-in-law George Burdett (who later married Ann) and Richard Parsons were witnesses to this event.[11] On the same day William also signed a bond for £2,000. A later addition to the document described it as a bond ensuring that William would make over the estate of their uncle Thomas to his brother (or else owe this large sum of money).[12] It is possible that Sir Robert's giving of the Kennedy's Lane houses and the Kildare land was in exchange for signing over his inheritance from his uncle, but another possibility hangs in the air.

The stripping of this inheritance from William would suggest that, sometime between 1 and 6 April, he had told his family that he had become a Catholic and was intending to become a Benedictine. Benedictine records show that William entered that community in August 1687, having been influenced by the preaching of Dom Joseph Johnston while he was at Lincoln's Inn.[13] This would probably have been the year in which he finished his legal training, it normally being a six-year stint. Such a choice on William's part would not have been kindly received in a staunchly Protestant family in the midst of a growing political crisis focused on religion. He had become *persona non grata* in his family.

Also in 1685, Frances gave birth to a second boy, Howard. This time, however, the child was very unwell and it would seem that Frances did not survive. Ralph Howard whisked the babe off to London to have the abdominal opening stitched, as it had not properly knit together before he was born. The operation was a success, and Howard survived the return journey. Now a widower with two very young sons, the complexion of Sir Robert II's world had changed painfully in the space of a year—his own *annus horribilis.*

With the lord lieutenant then a Catholic, Protestant distress in Ireland was growing rapidly. A significant number had fled to England, fearful of a Catholic backlash as had been seen in 1641. Sir Robert's brother-in-law, Bishop Edward Jones, was making plans to go as well. Robert II obtained a £600 loan from Capt. Matthew Ford, a relative through the Shanganagh Walshes, secured on fourteen townlands of the estate.[14] Next, he kept a coachman on a retainer, so that he could be ready to move at short notice.[15] In the end, sometime in 1687 he decided to go to the Isle of Man, regarded by some as a less contentious venue than England.

In a letter from Douglas, dated 25 February 1687/8, Sir Robert II handed over all his goods to Dr Ralph Howard, released his seneschal, Edmond Neill (Ned Neal), from his service, and asked that financial records of income and expenditures be kept. (It would appear that Robert II was the first to keep financial records on the estate, unless earlier efforts simply have not survived.) The letter, when folded, is seen to be addressed to Dr Howard at his Ship Street house[16] (Illus. 18). One would imagine that he sent other letters as well, but this is all we have. Apparently, Robert II was not well. Whether he had been

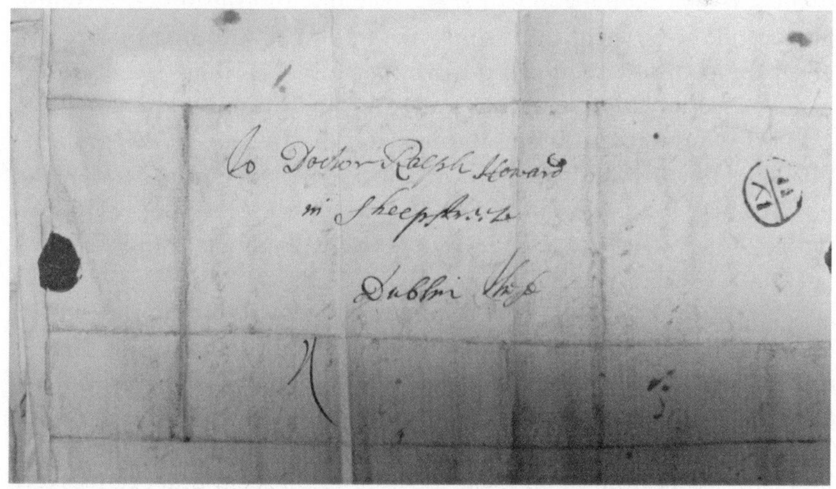

Illus. 18—Envelope addressed to Dr Howard, NLI, Wicklow Papers, MS 38,638/1.

severely injured or was suffering from a fatal illness is unclear. There is no hint in the records regarding his cause of death but die he did, on 2 April 1688.[17]

Fortunately, the seneschal was able to get to Sir Robert II before he passed, allowing him to make his last will and testament. Interestingly, this document does not survive. Surely it would have been an important item in the estate's papers—unless, of course, it was to someone's advantage that it did not remain? As part of this communication, Robert II had also requested that Dr Ralph Howard, the Revd Edward Jones, bishop of Cloyne, and Capt. Matthew Ford of Wexford take on the job of being the guardians of his young sons.[18]

For a period of time after Robert II's last letter, the only source of information from the Mount Kennedy point of view are letters from Edward Jones to Ralph Howard. From these we learn that Sir Robert II requested that he be laid next to his wife in the family vault in Delgany. This is our first indication that Frances had died before her husband. And, as so often happens in families, there was a split. Sarah and Gilbert Heathcote did not get on with Edward Jones. Given what mischief Jones is said to have been up to later, we can see that the situation was complex at best.

Jones also noted that Ralph Howard did not want to be the executor of Sir Robert's will. The fact that two heirs survived meant that there was very little hope of the Howards ever coming into the property with which they had parted, so there was 'no profit' to be had. This may seem a bit mercenary, but it was probably for the best that Ralph Howard did not accept this duty. Accusations of conflict of interest, given the complex financial transactions in which they had engaged, would have left him very vulnerable to any future legal challenges. Edward Jones was also hesitant to take on the role, but it can easily be imagined that his wife, Elizabeth Kennedy, persuaded him. After taking legal advice, Jones agreed to be the executor.[19] What Ralph Howard did do, however, was go to the Isle of Man and bring his grandsons back to Ireland.

The death of Sir Robert II Kennedy had also set in motion activity among the Benedictines in Paris, where William Kennedy was then in their novitiate, preparing to become a full member of the group. We are fortunate that there was a contemporary witness to these events. His name was Ralph Bennet Weldon; he was William's fellow novice and later the community's historian.

> 'WJK [William Joseph (his name in religion) Kennedy] sent to London in 1682 to Inns of Court … In this famous town he became a Roman Catholic … But his brother Sir Robert [II] Kennedy dying he was sent by his superiors into Ireland to look after his affairs[.] [W]hile he was thus busied King James II of glorious memory came into the country and empowered him to act for him on the Lands about his brother's estate, to raise soldiers, etc., and made him Governor of Wicklow, a Castle on the seashore.'[20]

This source provides us with some quite unexpected developments in the Mount Kennedy story. Certainly, there is no hint in other sources that William was ever made the governor of Wicklow Castle, but this does make sense of a blank instrument of appointment for a quartermaster found in the estate papers which corroborates Weldon's account.[21] The Benedictines were fierce Jacobites, and Dom Joseph Johnston, whose preaching triggered William's conversion, was one of James II's personal chaplains. Sending William back to his family's estate would have been seen as a good opportunity to swing it in James's favour.

Edward Jones's next letter to Ralph Howard, dated 2 October, was evidently written after William's arrival at Mount Kennedy. As one might expect, he was no fan of William's, and the news that the king had put him in charge of the estate did not please Edward. He cited the Gunpowder Plot, and said that William would 'accomplish some Notorious Villany & at least blow up his own Family'.[22] The Gunpowder Plot was a conspiracy by some Catholics to assassinate James I in 1605 and put his nine-year-old Catholic daughter on the throne. The plot was foiled but still echoed in the minds of Protestants. More to the point is the sense of threat to their guardianship of the heirs and their estate. The fear of losing control of the children was, however, well founded.

Edward's letter goes on to complain that his brother Matthew's wife, Bridget Kennedy Jones, has not received any money out of the estate, as she was meant to. This recalls the theme of a lack of money. Ralph Howard had told him that there had been a problem of the arrears of rent being stolen. But more than money was about to be stolen.

William was working closely with his sister Sarah. They were trying to manage the estate and find out where the money was going. It was evidently in disarray, as the estate manager was accused by the tenants of allowing £7,000 worth of improvements to the house and outbuildings to deteriorate.[23] Sarah was of a similar disposition to her brother. Her husband was the son of a Parliamentarian soldier and tended to Nonconformity. Minority religious followers, even when at different ends of a spectrum, can sometimes give the adherents a sense of being united in opposition. Perhaps together they hatched a daring plan in which he would take their brother's eldest boy, Sir Richard II, only a few months beyond his fourth birthday, to France and raise him as a Catholic.[24] From this distance in history, it strikes one as the ill-advised exuberance of a 27-year-old youth.

It is not known precisely where the two young boys would have been living. One possibility is with their Kennedy grandmother, as her brother George's name had been put forward as a possible guardian, but the most likely option is that they were with their Howard grandparents at their Ship Street house. William, on the other hand, was most probably living in the big house in Wicklow, though he could have been visiting at the Kennedy's Lane house where his mother was living. There is no indication how she had reacted to his becoming a Benedictine.

On 17 November, he set off with his nephew in front of him on his horse. How did he manage to get the boy in the first place? And how did the boy react to such a caper? Perhaps initially it was a great adventure, but the distance from Dublin to Drogheda is at least 53km (33 miles) and could not have been covered in one go. The child must surely have begun to tire of such a journey. On the other hand, William may have made use of friends' or religious houses as places of rest on his northward dash.

Soon enough the alarm was raised, and on the 26th one Bryan Fitzsimons was promised £50 if he could rescue the lad who had been spirited away.[25] A dozen or more men were quickly mustered and set off at a gallop, pursuing the kidnapper. They took a coach and driver with them to bring back William and the boy. The duo's progress must have been slow enough, because the posse managed to catch up with them in Drogheda. Or perhaps there were no ships sailing, November not being the best time for sailing from Ireland to England. Unfortunately, the coachman was killed in the escapade.[26] One can imagine the crowing of the captors and the verbal, if not physical, abuse that was heaped on William during the return journey. They made good time and were back in Dublin by the last day of November. Ralph Howard delivered the money to Bryan for the safe return of his grandson, and gave the coachman's widow £5.

Although Tyrconnell, the Catholic viceroy of Ireland, would have been sympathetic to William's impulse, he had to censure the young man lest there be a strong reaction from the Protestant population. He was not imprisoned, however, and continued to live at Mount Kennedy. Edward Jones, who had been William's headmaster at the Kilkenny school before he went to Trinity, had this to say about him early that December 1688:

> 'I need not [re]mind you that Will Kennedy is Will Kennedy still, base and treacherous to a Proverb, so you must not think the children secure without a guard; besides the Devil is most eager when his time is short, as I hope the continuance of [these? (torn off)] wicked spirits among us is.'[27]

This is ironic coming from a bishop who would later be fired by his church for all manner of corruption.

William stayed on for nearly two more years, however, eventually returning to France in November 1690. During this time William of Orange landed in England and James II made his way to Ireland, landing at Cork. He would have passed close by Mount Kennedy on his journey north towards Dublin. It would probably have been at this time that William would have met with James and been asked to raise soldiers, and been put in charge of the castle at Wicklow town, 16km south of the estate[28] (though it is unlikely that he ever actually set foot there).

Also during this time Sarah, with William's help, took a case against the guardians of their nephews, Ralph Howard and Edward Jones, who had taken the children to England. They said that this was to keep them safe from William, though it also fell in with the more general flight of Protestants at that time, perhaps serving two purposes. The Irish Parliament, however, had said that the estates of anyone leaving Ireland would be forfeit to the Crown. William therefore asked that new guardians be appointed because Mount Kennedy was adrift, falling into disrepair, and rents being syphoned off by an unscrupulous agent for the estate.[29] Ann Kennedy Burdett and Bridget Kennedy Jones were opposed to Sarah and himself, though they all agreed that the profits of the estate which should be coming to them were not. (Interestingly, there is no mention of Constance Kennedy Parry Seymour.)

Despite his best efforts, William does not seem to have been able to make much of a dent in the chaos of his family's estate. Later, a Bray court found him guilty of treason in 1703, and his houses on Kennedy's

Lane were confiscated and put up for auction.[30]

As previously noted, the Kennedy mansion on the demesne was evidently at least damaged in the Williamite wars, if not put beyond use. The Hearth Money Rolls tell us that in 1669, before its improvement, it had ten hearths. Unlike in the late 1640s, when the Kennedys managed to play both sides and transition unscathed through a change of government, this time, with members on both sides of the conflict, they lost out in both directions. Their house was probably damaged by local Williamite forces (or perhaps even by Jacobite ones). Because William's earlier attainder for serving James II was 'discovered' (revealed) to the Crown in the 1710s by his sister Elizabeth, the government took three-fourths of the rents of the estate.[31]

The 1690s were a very lean time at Mount Kennedy. The impact of the Williamite wars was severe. Real estate values plummeted, and returns from tenants also decreased, so that rents had to be reduced. Accounts had been kept but their accuracy was suspect. George Antrobus had been the agent when William Kennedy had been present. After him there was Joseph Hutcheson, and then John Ford (evidently not related to Matthew Ford). The guardians continued to renew leases and negotiate others. Ralph Howard kept all the receipts for every expense incurred by the Kennedy brothers and got his money back in the end, just before Sir Richard II came of age.

Both Sir Richard II and his brother Howard attended Trinity College (though not Lincoln's Inn), along with their Howard uncles with whom they had grown up. Ralph Howard had been in his late 30s when he started his family, so some of the uncles and the nephews were close in age. Howard Kennedy appears to have suffered from delicate health; he died sometime between 1707 (when his brother made his will) and 1710, when he would have been 25 years old. He had no offspring. His and his older brother's personalities are commented upon by his uncle Robert Howard, then a fellow of Trinity College, writing to his older brother, Hugh. The description is concise, capturing the entitled, ambitious and foolish self-centredness that afflicted so many of their class and generation.[32]

At the end of February 1704/5, another letter in the same exchange gives us the news of how Sir Richard II pursued his aspirations in England.

> 'I received yours, and am surprised at the account you give of Sir Richard's behaviour at his wedding which is very extraordinary and yet very agreeable to the absurdity with which he has

> managed that whole affair; my mother — received a letter from him lately wherein he talks very pompously of his new Alliance, and very confidently, of his wife's fortune, which he makes no doubt of receiving to the full, which if he ever does, Sir Francis [Sir Richard's father-in-law, Sir Francis Blake] is not the man I took him to be ...' [33]

Despite his unrealistic expectations, however, Sir Richard II could be dangerous. Two years later, there is evidence in the next surviving Howard letter that he had made a formidable effort to commandeer the Howards' estate when he came of age in 1706. He had gone back over the tripartite and other agreements that had been made at the time of his parents' marriage. From his reading of these, he had decided that he was entitled to the whole of the Howard estate as well as that of his father. As one might imagine, Ralph Howard and his family were in a sweat lest this be proved in court. There were numerous legal assessments of the documents involved, and in the end it was decided that Richard was not so entitled.[34]

Sir Robert II Kennedy's attention to detail in the drawing up of the pertinent documents proved very important 25 years later, but Sir Richard II should have been entitled to the land in the Wexford baronies of Gorey and Bargy. Nothing has been found in the records to indicate whether he indeed obtained them. Then again, Sir Richard's solicitor was his uncle on the Howard side, so it is unclear how impartial he was, though it was not he who made the assessments. It is also possible that these lands were returned to Ralph Howard in payment of the money owed by the Kennedys for his taking care of them as children. The Howards went on to become Earls of Wicklow, having narrowly missed being ruined at this stage.

Sir Richard II had married Katherine Blake of Oxfordshire. They were living in England and they had a daughter, Elizabeth, towards the end of 1705. In 1710 Sir Richard's sense of entitlement and recklessness propelled him to challenge a certain John Dormer to a duel, in which Richard was killed. (The surname Dormer would suggest an English Catholic.[35]) There is no word of where he was buried, though he had made a will, which was proved in Dublin in September 1713.[36] Mr Dormer was duly pardoned for the death which had resulted from the duel.[37] Katherine went on to marry a son of the Duke of Norfolk, Frederick Howard.

The copy of Richard II's will at the Dublin Registry of Deeds tells us that he left £350 per year to his widow, to be paid out of the income of the estate (as all further bequests were also to be sourced). He had hoped for a male heir but there was none, nor any heir 'from the body of' his brother Howard. Instead, he was obliged to leave all to his daughter, but only for her lifetime. Her offspring were to acquire the estate on reaching 21 years of age. If Elizabeth had no legal issue, then all his estate was to go to William Domville of the County of Dublin 'and all his heirs forever'.

This Domville connection is first seen when William's fourth son, Lancelot, was the manucaptor (the person who guarantees that the student will show up) for Robert II's entry into Lincoln's Inn in 1668. Given that Richard II would be unlikely to remember his father, his relationship to William (or perhaps William's son William) must have been nurtured by his Howard grandparents. Also out of the estate, Richard gave John Elmwood of Trinity College £100 a year for life, indicating that he had made a lasting friendship during his college years.

Richard's daughter was provided with £2,000 for her marriage portion, as well as a stipend of £100 a year until she turned fourteen, at which time she was expected to marry. Richard also made her the payee for the £5,000 which he said was owed to him by his father-in-law, Francis Blake. Richard evidently was very fond of his Howard grandmother. He gave her £100 as a token of 'his gratitude for her great care and tenderness she had for him in his Education'. He made Humphrey Matthews and John Elmwood his executors, with £20 for mourning clothes and rings. William Domville was likewise endowed.

Richard II's will evidences a relatively small circle of family and friends, with no connection to any of his cousins. He appears to have been adrift in the world in terms of significant relationships. In his case, the episodes of trauma in his life are multiple and profound. His mother died when he was only one year old. His father died a couple of years later, when they were living in a foreign place. At the age of four, he had been kidnapped by a man he hardly knew. (William had asked him for forgiveness when they met years later in London, and Richard assured him that there were no hard feelings.[38]) From an early age he was known as 'Sir Richard', which could easily have given him an inflated sense of his own importance.

Robert Howard's specific characterisation of Richard was as 'bubble-headed'. This term was used to indicate a foolish, stupid or disorganised person. The inability to focus in a functional way would also be consistent with someone who has been affected by trauma.

Trauma tends to throw the cerebral cortex off-line, as the threat had required a physical action rather than a thought-out response. The person appears ungrounded, not able to respond appropriately in the present moment. Indeed, his or her body is still stuck in the old event(s).

The fear physically residual in the body after severe trauma leaves a person grappling with much anxiety and distrust. If this happens when a person is old enough to remember the incident, he or she may be able to connect the two phenomena. Richard II's experience with William probably remained in his consciousness, but certainly not the death of his mother. It is only relatively recently, however, that we have come to understand the connection between trauma and its long-term retention in the human body.

This underlying distress would have seriously challenged Richard II's ability to mature emotionally. His bravado, entitlement and level of risk-taking are some of the ways in which very insecure people attempt to cope with life's earlier events. Unrealistic expectations of life shielded him from anxiety that he had no way of understanding. His social class allowed him to marry well, but it could not always protect him from the consequences of his rash actions. Without this significant level of trauma, he might have grown into a more functional adult. In a family that needed an emotionally mature heir to survive, he was almost certainly doomed to failure.

Richard II's daughter, Elizabeth, was only five years old when her mother became her guardian and the overseer of the Kennedy estate. Katherine continued in this role until Elizabeth married Sir William Dudley, who then took over these functions. Thus Elizabeth, daughter of Sir Richard II, grew up as English and married an English baronet.

After Sir Richard II's death in 1710, Elizabeth Kennedy Jones, daughter of the first Richard, began her long struggle to have the estate come to her rather than to her grand-niece, Lady Elizabeth Kennedy Dudley, daughter of Sir Richard II. The elder Elizabeth would have been aware that her brother had been attainted in April 1694 for his participation in the Williamite war on the side of James II. This made him ineligible to own the property. In 1713 Elizabeth received an acknowledgement of her petition to Queen Anne, in which she had reminded the queen of William's attainder and asked to be given the 'discoverer's' share of the estate.[39] Unfortunately, the queen died not long afterward, so Elizabeth had to restart the whole process. Later, her son, Robert Jones, also became involved in the legal battle for the estate.

It was not until the younger Elizabeth came of age in 1726, and therefore became the actual inheritor of Mount Kennedy, that the legal logjam began to shift again. It is in the title to the estate held by Robert Cunningham, Lord Rossmore, that we find outlined the history of property transactions leading to his ownership.[40] It tells us several important things. One is that Robert Jones had managed to get a lease (or *custodiam*) for the entire property from the Crown for 99 years in 1726[41] after his mother had died (which was sometime between 1714 and 1725). The *custodiam* was initially dependent on the continued survival of Dom William Kennedy. The Crown took three-quarters of the estate's rents because of Dom William's attainder, but Robert Jones, as his mother's executor and heir, received his mother's entitlement to the property as the 'discoverer'. He therefore continued to be the one in charge of the estate on the ground; he lived in Newtownmountkennedy in 1669 but moved to England in the 1700s.[42] He then bequeathed his lease to his younger cousin, Elizabeth Barker (the grand-niece of Ann Barker, Richard I's wife, by her brother George). She in turn sold it to Robert Cunningham in 1769 for nearly £20,000, shortly before her own death.[43] Robert Jones had heavily encumbered the *custodiam* with a number of mortgages to various parties in England.[44] For this reason, even though Elizabeth received a princely sum for it, most of that went to pay off the debts incurred by Robert over his lifetime. This is likely why it cost Cunningham such a great sum.

Sir William Dudley continued to hold ownership of the overall Kennedy estate into the 1740s (Robert Jones being the principal tenant), but he also had his own estate in England, over which he was heavily indebted. He was determined to sell Mount Kennedy to pay these debts[45] and did so, in July 1750, to Robert Mackey, a London merchant. The latter turned out to be a front man for Sir Peter Warren of Bath, evidently a property speculator. Sir Peter's widow sold it to Robert Cunningham in 1753[46] for nearly £17,000, and Cunningham held it until his death in 1801. The estate cost him nearly £40,000, when taking into consideration the cost of buying both the *custodiam* and the title. This is given as the reason why he was unable to start building his house there for another ten years after his purchase of the lease from Elizabeth Barker.

The Kennedys' fall from prominence on the Dublin scene was quite rapid after the death of Sir Richard I in 1684/5. His son, Robert II, may have been popular on Dublin's social scene, but in terms of political or economic significance there was nothing left. Richard's death was rapidly followed by the death of King Charles II, which resulted in considerable upheaval on a national level. Robert II was caught up in the panic of the property-owners who were his co-religionists. He had no patron in the Catholic-led Irish government, and no post or networking circle of any significance. He fled abroad, as did his father-in-law and one of his brothers-in-law. Bad luck overtook him, and the Kennedys disappeared from view as a family of note.

6
Tail-end

The ironies in history are many, and there are a number in this Kennedy story. The last male survivor of the Kennedys of Mount Kennedy was a Catholic and a Benedictine priest. It is likely that William was a complete mystery to most of his family. He would have grown up as the spare heir in a very well-off setting, the wealth of which would have shaped his early experience of life. He was sent to the prestigious Kilkenny school, where the headmaster would become his brother-in-law. After he did his BA at Trinity (and later an MA),[1] he went off to London and Lincoln's Inn in 1681, like the males of his line before him. His manucaptors there were two Englishmen, one from Middlesex and the other from Dorset,[2] indicating that his family had continued to cultivate English connections. These may have been connections of his mother, whose uncle was a lawyer.[3]

So, what in the preaching of Dom Joseph Johnston would have stirred him to consider converting to Catholicism, with all the implications of such a choice? At one point in a later letter, he mentioned that the two most important things in life for him were 'love of God and love of king'.[4] The Kennedys had become royalists to keep in step with the Restoration. William was a man of intense honesty and integrity, so perhaps he decided that the replacement of James II by William, the king's son-in-law, violated James's divine right to rule. This type of logic would also have supported a move to the 'true' church, which, again, had been a divine institution rejected by a man, even though that man was a king.

Whatever line of thought had led him to his decision, he knew that it was going to cost him. The loss of all his property and the Exchequer office that was meant to be his was just the beginning. He was outlawed for his support of James II, losing even the right to own property. He could not function at law and so lost his livelihood. Even within the

English Benedictine community he was not well liked, quite possibly owing to his title, his education and his Irishness. The head of the community, Dom Joseph Johnston, thought well of him, however, and so he was ordained in 1694 and assigned a number of offices within the community.[5]

In 1705, at the age of 44, Dom William Joseph was sent from Paris into England to serve with the English mission. At this time the government had an extensive network of spies, constantly trying to stay ahead of various plots by Jacobites to reinstate James II, and later, after he died in 1701, his son, James III. On 20 March 1710, through the efforts of Capt. Burk,[6] one of these spies, William was arrested and thrown into prison for being the Catholic archbishop of Dublin. There, although found not guilty of being the archbishop, he was still attainted for treason and suffered 'two long imprisonments'.[7] After his release, William continued to move between England and France, as required by his community.

It is not that Fr Kennedy did not know fear in acting on his convictions. In midlife he had become friends with a Mr Shortiss, who was himself a friend of Sir Robert Walpole (and, it has been suggested, another one of the spies in the network).[8] As the friendship between Kennedy and Shortiss deepened, one evening Kennedy broached the subject of the other man perhaps becoming a supporter of James III. Shortiss didn't take him seriously, and obviously thought no more about it. He evidently recognised it simply as the expression of one man's deeply, but peaceably, held point of view. That night, however, Kennedy had a definite reaction to the earlier conversation. As he wrote later to James III,

> 'As the Law, Sir, was my Education soon as we parted I begun Seriously to reflect on the having put my Life entirely in his power and if Shortiss did not Discover [reveal] so treasonable a proposition w[i]th in eight & fourty hours to a Privy Councill[o]r if possible, or to the Civil Magistrate, he woud be guilty of Misprison [the concealment] of High Treason, and if he Imparted it to Sr Robt, Sr Robt woud Incur the same Penalty if not discover it to the Kings Secretary of State or Privy Councell[o]r in twelve hours.
>
> I assure y[ou]r Majestie I Slept not a wink that Night ...'[9]

In addition to his activities for the Benedictines, Sir William was also involved in the ongoing negotiations concerning Mount Kennedy. He was asking Sir William Dudley for a £100 annuity as his part of the estate.[10] Because his aunt Elizabeth had petitioned the Crown about the estate, Parliament had become involved. In London he became a well-known figure owing to the newspapers reporting on his loss of estate as a result of his Jacobite activities. The ongoing legal battle was also a matter of public interest.[11]

Sir William Dudley's mother-in-law's connection to the Duke of Norfolk led Dudley to expect that he would get whatever he wanted from Parliament, particularly the House of Lords. Quite coincidentally, however, Sir William Kennedy, OSB, had become friends with the then prime minister, Sir Robert Walpole, who was much impressed with William's honesty and integrity, despite his obvious Jacobite sympathies. Walpole used his considerable influence to block Dudley's efforts in Parliament, which forced him to accept a more reasonable arrangement with Robert Jones and William Kennedy. Here is an excerpt from William's letter to James III detailing Walpole's comments:

> 'I most Humbly ask y[ou]r Majesties Pardon for so tedious an acc[oun]t of what Seems only my p[ar]ticular affair, But tis a Demonstration, Sir, of Sr Robts Ste[a]ddiness for three Sessions of Parliam[en]t, notwithstanding the Vast Int[e]rest made Against me. And as the Dutchess of Hamilton often told me, Sr Robt Said to her Grace Since he was in Business, he never was so Importuned as to a Bond on me, but pray tell him says Sr Robt his Cause is Just and he's a very Honest man & I never will Abandon him.'[12]

This is a strong character reference, much contrary to the opinion of Edward Jones.

Such an episode is also of interest to a wider audience because Sir Robert Walpole was known to be very diligent in his pursuit of Jacobites, who were primarily Catholics, when he was a government minister. His strong defence of the public good would have led people to think that he was anti-Catholic, but this story shows that in fact, when it was clear that a Catholic was no threat to England, his own integrity moved him to see that justice was done. The other possibility is that Walpole wanted to keep William sweet as a source of Jacobite goings-on.

Dom William Joseph Kennedy died in Paris in 1738, at the age of 77. The circumstance of his death was an unfortunately common one in those days. He had fallen asleep in his room with the candle still burning. As it spilled over onto his table, the contents became inflamed and he died of smoke inhalation.[13] Thus the last baronet of Mount Kennedy passed from this life. He would have been buried in the Benedictine graveyard in Paris. During the French Revolution this was emptied and all bones scattered. Nothing to see there either.

Conclusion

Having a middle-ranking family to explore in detail has offered us an opportunity to live through the seventeenth century with people on the ground. Although the Kennedys were Gaelic, giving them a connection with Irish-speakers and Catholics, at least some of them appear to have been thoroughly Anglicised by the late sixteenth century. Further, the head of this line may have been a radical Protestant, which would indicate a high degree of alienation from his ancestors. His Protestant affiliation gave him the opportunity to pursue greater wealth while others were losing theirs. For the vast majority of Gaelic Ireland, this century was chaotic and embattled, with a disastrous loss of land, culture and way of life. For those entrepreneurs coming from England, and those who joined them, it was a wonderful opportunity to make large amounts of money, establish a dynasty and gain titles.

Even for this group, however, there were many pitfalls and deadly developments. It was a case of survival of the luckiest as much as of the fittest. The extant documents of the Kennedy estate illustrate both experiences. Significantly, Robert Kennedy had suffered the impact of traumatic events as a child. This appears to have enhanced his 'fight' response, and he was aggressive in his pursuit of power and wealth. Even when confronted by immense setbacks—such as being fired from his powerful job, having his estate devastated by the 1641 rebellion or losing his wife and heir to the plague in the early 1650s—he persisted, and achieved a title and a manor. His great-grandson, on the other hand, in a very different context but also suffering from the effects of trauma, was unable to muster sufficient focus or emotional maturity either to make wise choices or to survive.

The Gaelic clans had indeed been facing a no-win situation if they had hoped to keep their culture, their religion or their land. The advice to 'join them if you can't beat them' was taken to heart by a small percentage, especially those who had previously achieved some measure of financial success. Robert Kennedy would have belonged to this small cohort in the early part of the century, and he was determined to expand the family fortunes. Given the centrality of the English legal system to the colonising effort, he sought out powerful people who could facilitate his entry into it. With cover from above, he pushed resolutely, gambling by borrowing, to finance his growing property portfolio within Dublin. Then, after experimenting with land ownership in various ways and locations, and having achieved a lucrative court post, he focused his efforts on the recently shired county of Wicklow.

The late sixteenth century and the first third of the seventeenth saw a Wild West show of land-grabbing from the Gaelic clans. By adopting the guise of an English adventurer, Robert Kennedy was able to use both Gaelic techniques and English mortgages to acquire a sizeable amount of land in Wicklow. His manner of conducting himself, reflecting his mentor William Parsons, was one of deceit, aggressive moneylending and networking with powerful people. He also benefited from legal immunity thanks to his court post. When challenged on his duplicity, he merely denied that it had ever happened. His style of doing business does not inspire one with admiration but it achieved his ends.

Even with this careful game plan, his efforts would have been in vain if he had not been positioned to profit from the disasters inflicted on his relatives near and distant. It was his gaining of the chief remembrancer's post with its enhanced income as well as the major part of Alderman Kennedy's fortune that allowed him to beat the competition in Wicklow and gradually take over a goodly number of the townlands in Newcastle barony. His new-found wealth gave him the means to make loans to the Wicklow Irish, which he knew they could not repay. This skilful use of mortgages was the main instrument by which he took the land for himself.

By the time Thomas Wentworth arrived on the scene, throwing a spanner into the 'business as usual' practices of the élites, Kennedy had acquired enough land to make a living from English-style agriculture along with his rental incomes. When Wentworth had sufficiently shaken things up, the Gaelic and even Old English landowners registered the English government as a serious threat to their continued well-being. They joined forces to fight back after the 1641 rebellion got under way.

Various factors thwarted a reasonable outcome, most significantly the aggressive underhandedness of William Parsons. Developments in England then interposed themselves on the flow of events, and civil war erupted there. Radical Protestant Parliamentarians executed the king and pursued their own agenda. The soldiers of war demanded payment, and Ireland was the obvious source.

Nevertheless, Robert Kennedy was well positioned to keep his land. He had invested in legal training for his sons so that they could continue to rise in that profession. His son Richard was able to find acceptance among the re-emerging Royalist supporters. Robert and Richard helped to facilitate the restoration of the king and were rewarded with land, honours and Exchequer posts. They were confirmed as integral players on the national scene and appeared secure members of the élite.

But newly arrived players can never really take their place closer to the top for granted. Developments in England undermined the Kennedys' continued success. Now that the English more securely controlled Ireland, there was not the same need to pay attention to their officials in Dublin, who thus lost influence. The further cultivation of powerful friends and promoters was much more difficult owing to their local scarcity. The smart money had gone to London, where the ear of the king was nearer to hand.

On top of this, the younger Robert Kennedy was simply unlucky. His wife died in childbirth, and he died young as well, falling foul of more chaos emanating from England. He had decided to entrust his heirs to his in-laws rather than to his own family. This left his estate at the mercy of uninterested parties, and his sons lacked either the health to survive or the maturity required to navigate the usual political and social gauntlets. The family line limped to an English end and the estate was sold. The remaining baronet had turned his back on the family's lifestyle and sought to live honourably and honestly, not only as a Catholic but also as a Benedictine priest.

As previously mentioned, William Kennedy had a very different set of values from the baronets who preceded him. There is no adequate explanation for this phenomenon whereby a family member follows a very different path in life. William was not naïve about the cost of his choices, as is seen in his anxiety about possibly being turned over to the authorities yet again after his conversation with Shortiss, but he was a very honest man and was recognised as such by people of integrity.

The high point of the manor of Mount Kennedy was its creation in

1664, along with the baronetcy. Yet within not much more than a generation these Kennedys had ceased to function in any meaningful way in the affairs of Wicklow or Ireland. The estate was sold and they were gradually forgotten. It is rare that we have a chance to recoup local history from this period. The main dynamics had been constant pressure from men with money, buying out the land from under people and using the courts to dispossess others. In addition, there was pressure from men with the moral conviction that they were superior to those who did not share their religious point of view, killing anyone they considered illegitimate or heretical. All of this made the survival of documents from those times very difficult. Hopefully this book has gone some way towards restoring to public awareness this local, yet fairly uncommon, story within seventeenth-century Ireland.

Finally, in addition to a better understanding of Ireland in the seventeenth century, it is hoped that this work will restore an awareness of these Kennedys both to the people of County Wicklow and to historians of this period. While there are passing references to them in some books, and larger passages in studies of judges, their participation in the affairs of that century has never been fully elaborated. As a family, they contributed to the unfolding of history and are entitled to have their story told.

Appendices

Appendix A

From
The Complete Baronetage
by G.E. Cokayne (Exeter, 1900),
vol. 4, pp 196–7

KENNEDY[1]
cr. 25 Jan. 1664/5;[2]
forfeited 1710;
ex. Shortly after 1727 [1738]

i 1665 ROBERT KENNEDY, of Ballygarvey, *otherwise* Mount Kennedy, co. Wicklow,[3] first son of Robert Kennedy, was Joint Chief Remembrancer of the Exchequer [I.], 1625–34; Sheriff of co. Wicklow, 1643; M.P. [I.] for the borough of Kildare, 1643–49, and was created a Baronet [I.], by patent, dated 25 Jan. 1664/5,[4] which, however, was never enrolled, as neither were the King's Letters, but the Privy Seal was dat. 28 Oct. 1663 [*Carte Papers*]. He married firstly, probably before 1620, Con-

[1] The information in this article has been entirely furnished by G.D. Burtchaell. … There is a very incorrect pedigree of the family in Burke's *Patrician*, vol. v.

[2] List of Baronets in Ulster's office.

[3] The description (as well as the dates) of the grantees of these Irish Baronetcies is, in most cases, placed within inverted commas as being taken from the *Liber Munerum Publicorum Hiberniae* … . This, however, is not the case in this instance, inasmuch as the creation of 'Kennedy' has been omitted in that work.

[4] List of Baronets in Ulster's office.

stance, first daughter of Jonas Silyard, of Dublin, by Margaret, daughter of Ralph Sankey, of Fassaroe, co. Dublin. He married secondly (as her 4th husband), Elizabeth, widow (as 2nd wife) of Randoph Barlow, Archbishop of Tuam (d. 22 Feb. 1637), formerly wife of John Tanner, Bishop of Derry (d. 14 Oct. 1615), and before that, of the Rev. Luke Chaloner, D.D., Vice Chancellor of the Univ. of Dublin (d. 27 April 1613), daughter of Christopher Perceval. She d. s.p. 30 Jan. and was buried 3 Feb. 1658/9, at St Nicholas' Dublin. Funeral entry. He died March 1667/8, and 'was buried in the country.' Funeral Entry. Admon. [I.] 11 June 1677, to a creditor.

ii 1668 SIR RICHARD KENNEDY, Baronet [I. 1665] of Mount Kennedy aforesaid, 2nd but first surviving son and heir[5] by first wife, admitted to Lincoln's Inn, London, 25 Aug. 1638, and to the King's Inn, Dublin 28 Jan. 1656; was M.P. for Mullingar, 1647–49; *Knighted* 29 Aug. 1660, being made 27 Sept. Following, Joint Chief Remembrancer of the Exchequer [I.] and 8 Nov. in the same year, Second Baron of the Exchequer [I.], an office he resigned in 1681. He succeeded to the Baronetcy[6] in March 1667/8. He married about 1650, Anne, daughter of Christopher Barker, by Sarah, daughter of Bonham Norton. He, in 1682, settled Mount Kennedy and his other land in tail male. He died Jan. 1684/5.[7] Funeral entry. Will dated 19 Feb. 1679/80, proved 8 Sept. 1701, in Prerog. Court [I.]. The will of his widow dated 10 Jan. 1698/9, proved there 15 Oct. 1703.

iii 1685 SIR ROBERT KENNEDY, Baronet ..., of Mount Kennedy aforesaid, 1st son and heir, born about 1650; entered Trinity College, Dublin, as a Fellow Commoner, 23 Feb. 1665/6, aged 15; admitted to Lincoln's Inn, London, 9 Feb. 1670/1; succeeded to the Baronetcy, Jan. 1684/5; was Sheriff of co. Wicklow, 1686.[8] He married (Lic 20 Oct. 1682) Frances,

---

[5] His elder brother, Silvester Kennedy was admitted to Lincoln's Inn, 8 March 1630/1 by spec. favour. He married Mary, daughter of William Crofton, but died s.p. and v.p. His widow married (as his 3rd wife) Sir Paul Davys, Sec. of State [I.].

[6] He is called 'Sir R. Kennedy, Bart. [apparently a mistake for 'Knight'] Second Baron,' etc., in Royal letters, dated 3 Oct. 1662. [Smyth's *Law Officers of Ireland*, 1839, p. 154.]

[7] The statement in *Notes and Queries* [8th S., vi. 15] that the 2nd Baronet died in London, 10 May 1703, and was buried at St Margaret's, Westminster, is clearly an error. He is stated in the printed claim of Sir Wm. Dudley to the Kennedy estate to have died in 1684, and his son, the 3rd Baronet, in 1688.

[8] 'If to be judged by his intimates, extremely Whiggish.' [D'Alton's 'King James' Irish Army List,

sister of Robert Howard, Bishop of Elphin [1729–40], daughter of Ralph Howard of Shelton Abbey, co. Wicklow, by Catherine, daughter of Roger Sotheby. He died 1688. Funeral entry.

iv 1688 SIR RICHARD KENNEDY, Baronet ... of Mount Kennedy aforesaid, to 1st son and heir; born there about 1686; succeeded to the Baronetcy in 1701; entered Trinity College, Dublin, 22 Jan. 1703/4 aged 16. He, when of full age, suffered a recovery of the entailed estates, thereby vesting them in himself absolutely. He was Sheriff of co. Dublin, 1709. He married Katherine, daughter of Sir Francis Blake of Oxfordshire. He died s.p.m.,[9] aged 23, being killed in a duel, by Mr Dormer in April 1710. Will dated 22 July 1707, proved at Dublin 25 Sept. 1710. His widow married Lord Frederick Henry Howard (younger son of Henry, Duke of Norfolk), who died 16 March 1726/7, aged 42. She died 22 Jan. 1731/2.

v 1710 SIR WILLIAM KENNEDY, Baronet ..., uncle and heir male, being to 2nd son of the 2nd Baronet; b. 1664; entered Trinity College, Dublin, 19 Jan. 1678/9, aged 14; MA, 1686. Being an adherent of James II, he was *attainted* 3 April (1694), 6 and 7 William and Mary, and, consequently, when *he became heir to the Baronetcy* in April 1710, was not legally entitled thereto. He became a monk in the English Monastery at Paris, and was living in France in 1727. On his death the *Baronetcy* presumably became *extinct.*

[https://archive.org/details/completebaroneta04coka/page/196/mode/2up; accessed 22 January 2018]

Ibid., vol. 3, pp 100–1

DUDLEY
created 1 Aug. 1660
extinct 15 June 1764

1689,' where also, among the outlawries of 1691, occurs the name of 'William Kennedy, of Mount Kennedy, co. Wicklow, popularly called Lord William Kennedy'.]

[9] Elizabeth, his only daughter and heir, married 12 Dec. 1719, Sir William Dudley, 3rd Baronet [1600], who died s.p. [?] 1764, aged 67, having previously advanced a claim to the Kennedy estates.

I 1660 'William Dudley of Clopton [*otherwise* Clapton] co Northampton, Esq,'[10] 2nd son of Edward Dudley, of the same (d. 6 May 1632, aged 62) by Elizabeth, daughter of Robert Wood, of Lamley, Nottsh., succeeded his elder brother, Edward Dudley, who d. s.p.m., 14 Nov. 1641, and *created* a *Baronet,* 1 Aug. 1660. ...

II 1670 Sir Matthew Dudley, Baronet, ... first son and heir by 3rd wife; succeeded to the baronetcy 18 Sept 1670 ...

III 1721 Sir William Dudley, Baronet ... of Clapton aforesaid, only son and heir b. there 2 March 1696; *succeeded to the Baronetcy,* 13 April 1721. He married 12 Dec. 1719, in London, Elizabeth, daughter and heir of Sir Richard Kennedy, 4th Baronet ... of Mount Kennedy, co. Wicklow[11] by Katherine, daughter of Sir Francis Blake. Her will dated 9 July 1747, proved 9 Feb. 1749/50. He died s.p.s.[12] at York, 15 June 1764, aged 68, when the *Baronetcy* became *extinct.* Will proved 1764.

[https://archive.org/details/completebaroneta03coka/page/100/mode/2up; accessed 22 January 2018]

[10] The manor of Clapton was held by the Dudley family from 1395, when Richard Dudley held it in right of his wife, Joan, daughter and heir of Robert Hoto, descended from Alfred de Grauntkort, who was said to have possessed it about 1090.

[11] The entail of this estate had been barred by her father, but inasmuch as the remainder man (under the entail to heirs *male*) was then under forfeiture, there was a lawsuit to decide as to whether the reversion had not been previously forfeited.

[12] Of his four children, three (O'Brien, William, and Elizabeth) died in infancy, while one, John, died v.p. and unmarried.

Appendix B
Dublin in the seventeenth century

Seventeenth-century Dublin was very different from the city we know today, and even in that century there was significant change throughout, as a very different group of people took control of it politically and socially. Physically, a river called the Poddle had originally run outside the town walls on the south-eastern side, flowing eastwards from just west of St Nicholas Gate and helping to defend the town. Early in the seventeenth century some of it had already been covered, so that the bridge which a sixteenth-century traveller would have met when emerging from St Nicholas Gate was no longer necessary. Just a few hundred feet to the east, however, the bridge in front of St Werburgh's (or Pole) Gate was still required.

Continuing along the walls to the east, there were no more gates, owing to the steep rise of the promontory on which the castle is built. The Poddle continued to form a natural barrier until it met an inlet of the Liffey, where an opening, known as Dame's Gate, had been erected. The name was derived from the church of Sainte Maria del Dam, which stood there from at least the twelfth century. There was, in fact, a dam at this point, helping to keep a steady water-level for defensive purposes rather than fluctuating with the tidal Liffey. Emboldened by the Reformation and his rapidly increasing wealth, Richard Boyle tore the church down in 1600 and built himself a large townhouse on the site. Today, Dublin City Hall occupies this plot of land. It was then at the easternmost boundary of the city, something to reflect on the next time you stand there.

Internally, the density of buildings increased, as numerous gardens gave way to the ever-increasing demand for housing and shops. In addition, the housing stock, especially on the smaller streets, was transformed from simple thatched cottages to cagework houses of two or more storeys. There were also more buildings of stone and, later, brick. Gradually the city's gates and walls were done away with. Although not a map of fine detail, Phillips's effort in 1685 indicates that the Poddle had been almost entirely built over and the east wall of the city had disappeared. The covering of the Poddle allowed the city to expand rapidly eastwards, with buildings lining Dame Street, which then connected what had been the eastern gate of the walled city with 'the Colledge', as Trinity was then known.

Dublin's water-supply was provided by the Poddle prior to the

Illus. 19—One of Dublin's medieval water conduits or fountains.

thirteenth century. After that it came from the Dodder, which was partly diverted above the Templeogue bridge, running as a stream until it reached St Thomas's Abbey. This area is a higher part of the ridge on which Thomas Street, High Street and Castle Street sit, allowing the water to flow down the incline, first in a wooden trough and then via a lead pipe. It was accessed through 'conduits' or public dispensing fountains along this ridge. As time went on, pipes were added to bring it directly into some of the houses. There were also a few smaller streams on the flatter area closer to the Liffey, which supplied some of the houses along Cook Street. Henry Berry's 1891 article, 'The water supply of ancient Dublin', makes very interesting reading, as he explains the details of its development. He includes a drawing of a conduit, which was located near St Audoen's church in the Corn Market (see Illus. 19).

Interestingly, there was apparently no sectional distinction between the well-off and the 'poorer sorts', as they were known. While High Street was acknowledged to be the most fashionable address, families of distinction also lived on Skinners Row, Castle Street, St Nicholas Street, Copper Alley, Cook Street and Merchants Quay. It is more probable, however, that the wealthy lived on the main streets, while the less-well-off lived in smaller houses on the back lanes. They would have been recruited as servants for the townhouses of the well-off, as well as being petty traders and tradesmen. Later in the century, High Street lost its clientele to the suburbs and its polish faded.

Early in this century, alehouses and wine taverns were very numerous. Indeed, the cellars under Christ Church Cathedral were rented out to vintners after the Reformation, noticeably compromising the atmosphere of the space above. In the second half of the century, the number of booksellers and printers gradually rose, especially after the Restoration, when commerce and money once again flowed freely. It was probably only in the last two decades that coffee-houses made an appearance, but when they did they were immensely popular. One of them was in the repurposed Cork House, and another was on Skinners Row.

In effect, at the beginning of the seventeenth century Dublin was a medieval walled town, while by 1700 it had become one of the leading cities of Ireland, England and Scotland, having incorporated many areas once beyond the walls.

(Unless otherwise specified, this information comes from J.T. Gilbert's *The History of the City of Dublin* (Dublin, 1854), vol. 1, and Howard Clarke's *Irish Historic Towns Atlas No. 11: Dublin, Part I, to 1610* (Dublin, 2002).)

Appendix C
The Christ Church complex

When we look at Christ Church Cathedral today, we see an impressive remnant of a building that has undergone significant changes over the eight centuries of its existence. When the stone version was first built in the twelfth century, a community of Augustinian Canons Regular would have been resident there. Canons were priests who lived in community but served the spiritual needs of the surrounding Christian community, unlike the more self-contained monastic communities that traditionally had been centred on prayer and manual labour and not all of whom were ordained.

The canons' living quarters and offices would have been built on to the south side of the cathedral, extending most of the way up the hill towards what was then Skinners Row. With the dissolution of religious communities in the 1530s, it was initially anticipated that the canons of Christ Church would suffer the same fate. Owing to the historic importance of the building and the centrality of its services to Dublin, however, it was decided that they would instead become secular canons, still ordained in the Anglican community but no longer under vows of poverty, chastity and obedience. The prior was replaced by a 'dean', and the canons were able to own personal property and to marry.

After a number of decades they no longer lived in community within the Christ Church complex, instead finding accommodation with their wives and children in the surrounding city. This left a number of empty rooms that no longer served a purpose and were deteriorating. When in the last years of the sixteenth century it was decided to move the Four Courts out of Dublin Castle, these empty rooms were converted to house them. This saved money, as adapting the extant buildings was much less expensive than constructing a new court centre. By 1608 the staff and records of the courts had taken up residence in this suite of rooms and cellars.

The prior's chambers, the refectory (a communal dining room), kitchen and cloister (an unroofed grassy square, bordered all round by a covered walkway), along with the cellars beneath them, were converted into rooms for King's Bench, Common Pleas, Chancery and the Exchequer. Because the rooms had not been originally designed for this purpose, they were at differing levels. Despite the lack of light, the cellars beneath became the offices of the chamberlains of the Exchequer. One smaller map of this area indicates a place that was

Illus. 20—View of the area of the Four Courts in Christ Church (NLI, ET A242, *Gentleman's Magazine*, April 1788; digital copy, used with permission).

specifically for the second chamberlain. This is where Robert Kennedy would have sat from 1608 until he was promoted to chief chamberlain in 1612 (see Illus. 5).

The living area of the canons had been accessed by an entrance on Christ Church Lane. This led into a dark passage that made its way through a maze of contiguous buildings, giving access to Christ Church Yard (originally a place of burial) and emerging eventually onto Fishamble Street. It was so dark and foreboding that it was known as the entrance to Hell. With the passage of time, it was decided that the court area needed improving and this was carried out in 1695. The drawings of the Four Courts that survive show these upgraded details and so are not exactly as they would have been in the time of the Kennedys, although they are probably not much different (see Illus. 20).

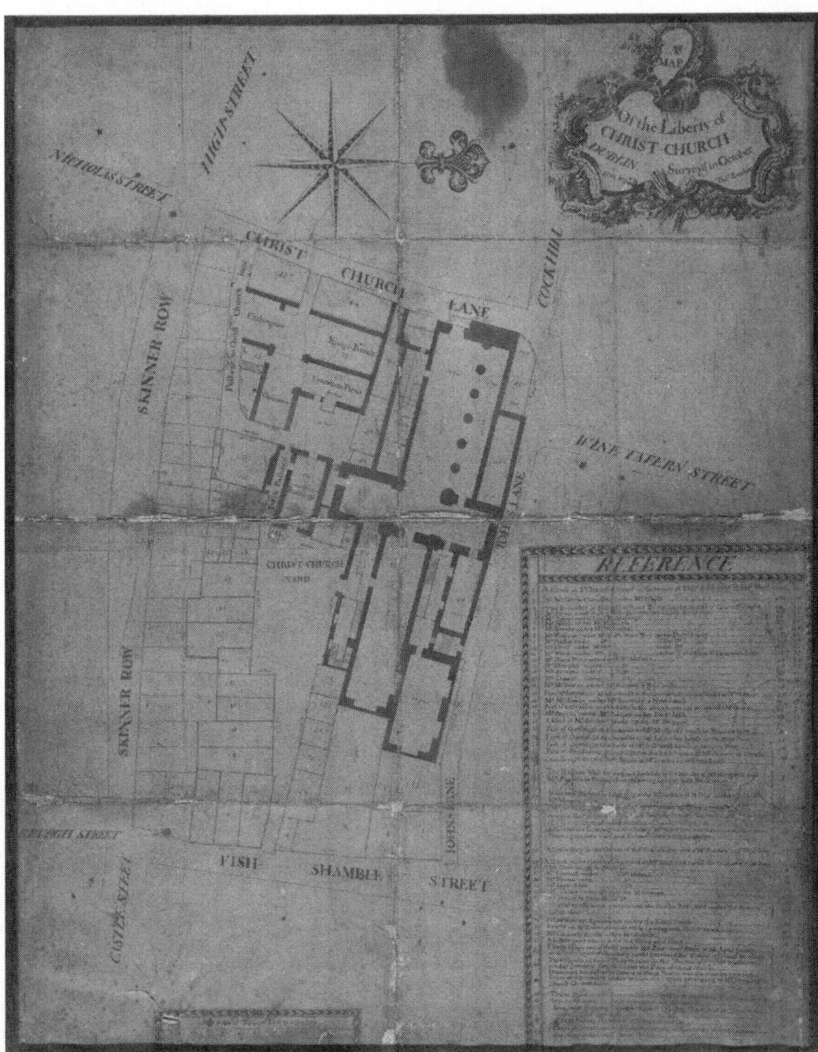

Illus. 21—Drawing of the Christ Church complex, including the transcribed key (RCB Library C6/3/2; Christ Church Liberty map showing the Four Courts, 1720s; used with permission).

Table 1—References for the above Christ Church Liberty map giving the names of the people in the various dwellings and spaces

	Front	Depth
1. A house in Fishamble Street in the tenure of William Anderson by Capt Sheaf	24½	30
2. Mr Willcocks Chandler under Mr White	24½	30

	Front	Depth
3. The Bulls head in Fishamble Street Philip Stapleton under Councellr Cooper	48	93
4. Mr Patens house built over the gateway into Christ Church yard	18½	22
5. Mr Connolly under Lord Russborough	16	46½
6. Mr Woods under Mr Wilkinson	15	46½
7. Mr Kennedy under Mr Wilkinson	15	46½
8. Mr Woodburn under Mr William Stern Noy under Doctr Brady	16½	48
9. Mr Hacket under Mr William Stern Noy under Doctr Brady	16½	48
10. Mr Davis under Mr Holt under Doctr Brady	16	37
11. Mr Walsh under Mr Holt under the Heirs of Erasmus Cope	16	37
12. Mr Davis Watchmaker under Mr Moland	16	20
13. Mr Murphy under Mr Moland	16	42
14. Mr Savage under Mr Moland	16	42
15. Mr Connor under Mr Moland	24	35
16. Mr McGowan under Mr Pultney a New house	15	17½
17. Pt of Coolfabius* as a backside to ye above house not yet leased to Mr McGowan	15	7½
18. Mr McGowan under Mr Poultney a New house		
19. [same as no. 17]	20	7½
20. Mr Copson under Mr Poultney under Doctor Jebb	18	13
21. A Shed in Mr Copsons hands under Mr Pultney	12	11
22. Part of Coolfabius as a backside to Mr Mullock's house in Skinner Row	8	11
23. Part of Coolfabius as a backside to Mr Lametres house in Skinner Row	12	11
24. Part of Coolfabius as a backside to Mr. Sillcock's house in Skinner Row	16	11
25. Part of Coolfabius given light to the back Rooms of Mr Connor in Christ Church Yard and the Back Rooms of Mr Irwins in Skinner Row	15	11
26. The Precinct Wall serving as a backside to the Houses of Mr Wingfield and Mrs Parsons in Skinner Row and given light to their Back Rooms	4	22
27. Shops and Tenements belonging to the Prebendary of St John in the tenure of Mr Morgan	36	32
28. The Old Exch[ange] in the tenure of Mr Conner		

	Front	Depth
under Mr Poulteny	25	50
Over the Exchange is a house built fronting Christ Church yard in the tenure of several under the Heirs of Erasmus Cope	25	30
Allso over the Exchange at the Rear of Mrs Copes house is the Chancellors Chamber Fronting the little yard and Extending over a Dark passage	40	20
29. A Little Shop in the Tenure of the Widow Bates under Mr Pultney under Dr Jebb	7¾	8½
30. A House in the tenure of the heirs of Mr Matthews under the Prebend of St Michan	20½	16
31. The Place where the Stocks is [sic]	9	10
32. Mr Cormack under Mr Moland	18	18
33. Mr Brown under ditto	16	18
34. Mr Crab under. ditto	16	18
35. Mr Tallon under Mr Holt by Mortgage	15½	18
36. Mr Jackson under ditto	30½	18
37. Mr McGowan's house underneath the Common Pleas held under the Dean of Christ Church	40	24
38. Mr McGowan Apar[t]ments under the Kings Bench	30	24
39. Vaults in McGowans hands with a passage into Christ Church lane	11	24
40. Mr Connor's house under Mr Fennor	22	16
41. A Little yard where there is a Water pipe fixed	8	14
42. Three shops one of them under the Four Court Steps with Apartments under the Court of Chancery in the tenure of William Ogle under Mr Throp	45	35
43. Two Houses in Christ Church lane in the Tenure of Mr Walldron under Co[u]ncellor Smith under the Dean of Christ Church	37	24
44. Chambers belonging to the Courts of Kings Bench and Exchequer and to the Court of Admiralty under which are	59	25
45. Three Houses with shops on Cock hill held by several tenants under Sr Caleb Smally	38	15
46. Ground formerly in Shops since taken into the Church	57	15
47. Shed Shops running the whole length of St Mary's Chapel held in Six Tenements under [illegible] Ogle Esqr	67	63
48. A Yard joining the Steps of St Marys Chapel	61	45
49. Shops in Johns Lane with back tenaments [sic] held under the William Anderson Deriving under Capt. Sheaf Deceased	30	40

*'Colfabius' was a medieval German surname. However, in this instance it appears to refer to something like a light well at the back of the houses that front onto Skinners Row.

A 1764 map of the complex shows the extent of the buildings and passages by that date. The reference guide on this map tells us that the various spaces depicted were occupied by private houses, wine taverns, alehouses and shops (such as for candles or a watchmaker), while some were still connected to the courts. The space was densely crammed, with some rooms built over the access passages and others being newly built, though perhaps these replaced some that had fallen asunder. The old Exchange, the place where merchants met every day to conduct business at the ringing of a bell, was also located here. The stocks, used for punishment, had a place, along with a small yard in which was located the all-important water-pipe (see Illus. 21).

To further increase the density of humanity frequenting this complex, houses of at least two storeys had been built directly in front of the Christ Church complex along Skinners Row. The rear of these houses would have been very dark, though some of them had negotiated light wells to alleviate this situation. The buildings were generally owned by wealthy men who then leased spaces to others, who sometimes went on to sublet in turn. The largest space was the Bull's Head tavern, with 48ft of frontage and extending 93ft to the rear. The smallest was a mere 8ft square, the size of a box room!

Skinners Row, no more than 17ft wide from house front to house front, had been further narrowed by vendors building out their fronts for the sale of goods, so that its width dwindled to only 12ft. A stoppage often ensued when two carriages or wagons met in this street. It was quite the bottleneck in the middle of the city's primary thoroughfare.

By the early nineteenth century the Wide Streets Commissioners had purchased most of the accretions to the original church complex, which were destroyed to allow for street-widening. Christ Church Lane became an extension of Winetavern Street, and the much-enlarged and rerouted Skinners Row became the very wide Christ Church Place, to the relief of many. The south face of the cathedral then became visible for the first time in centuries. The Four Courts were moved to their current home in 1796.

Appendix D
St Nicholas Street

Despite its relative brevity, St Nicholas Street (Illus. 22) contained two significant buildings. The first, the Tholsel, was located at the south-east corner of the intersection of Skinners Row to the east and High Street to the west, with Christ Church Lane running down the opposite side of the ridge. It had stood on this location since the fourteenth century. The name derived from two old English words, *toll* (tax) and *sael* (hall)—the place where tolls were paid. It served as court-house, custom-house and guildhall, and as a meeting place for merchants and the government at various stages. In 1597 it already suffered from a cleft in its eastern wall, which was further exacerbated by the gunpowder explosion in that year. It evidently was rebuilt a number of times, one of these being in 1683 and again in 1791, before it was levelled in the early nineteenth century (see Illus. 7).

The accompanying illustration shows the 1683 version, with an open but sheltered area on the ground floor and meeting rooms on the first floor. According to one traveller in 1697, it also provided a viewing platform from which the whole city could be seen. It was expanded in the seventeenth century by taking in some of the land that had previously been the burial yard for St Nicholas's Church, as well as the house to the east. As mentioned in the text, the trial of Robert Kennedy in 1633 was moved here from the Four Courts in Christ Church on the Saturday.

The next important building on this street is the one from which it took its name. St Nicholas was a fourth-century bishop in the Greek city of Myra on what is now the south-west coast of Turkey. His grave became a pilgrimage site for those from the eastern half of Europe, and he was especially dear to merchants and sailors. In the eleventh century his body was stolen by some sailors and taken to Italy, whence his veneration spread to the rest of Europe. The Anglo-Norman bishop John Cumin established the Church of St Nicholas Within the Walls in the twelfth century, probably with the help of local merchants looking for some assurance of safety on their sea voyages.[1]

The parish always struggled with a lack of funds. The building was redone in 1573, but the drawing that we have is from the 1707 rebuild (and thus not the church that the Kennedys would have known). The current remnant is from this time. Despite the rebuilding, the edifice continued to deteriorate for lack of maintenance. It was scheduled to

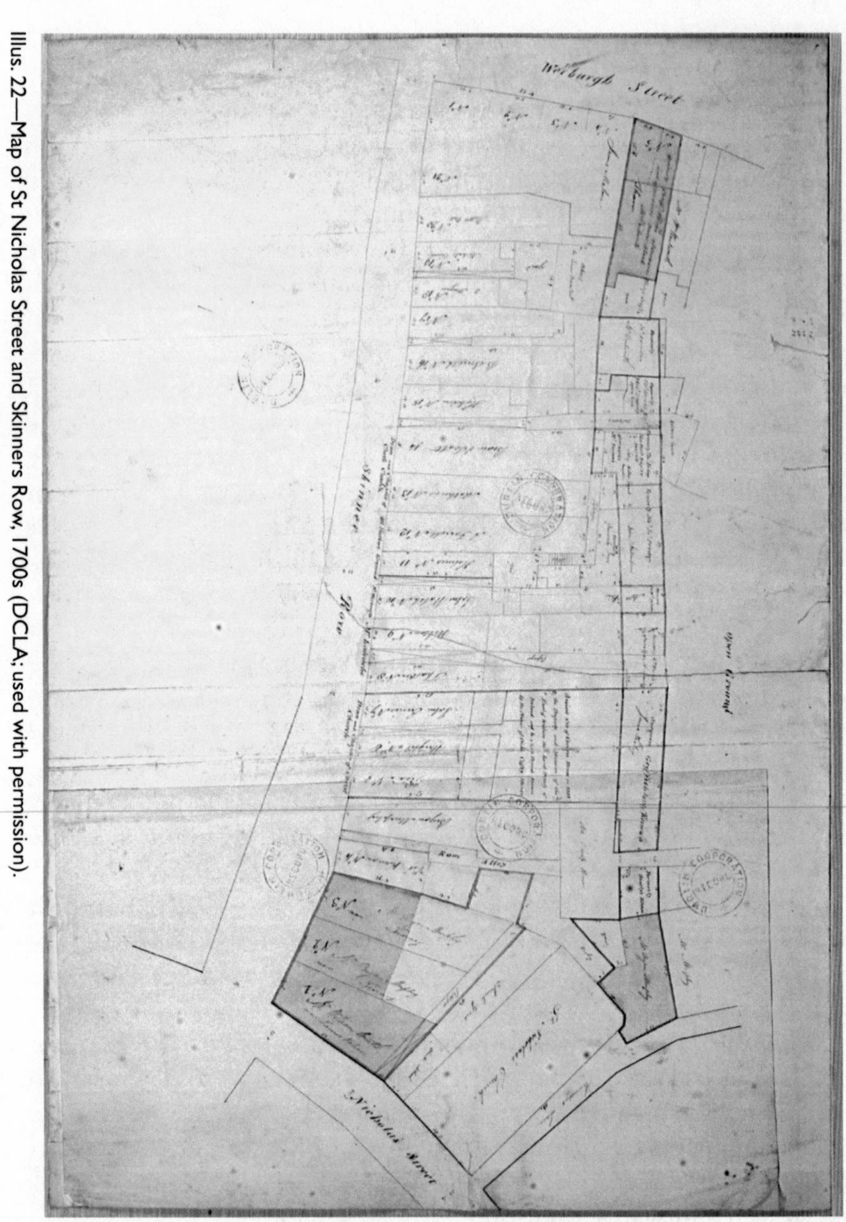

Illus. 22—Map of St Nicholas Street and Skinners Row, 1700s (DCLA; used with permission).

be demolished, but this did not occur in any organised way. A picture of the façade from the early twentieth century shows its original location further out onto the street, as well as the cobblestoned surface (see Illus. 23–25).

Robert Kennedy's first wife, Constance Sulliard, and their eldest son,

Illus. 23—St Nicholas's church, protruding into the footpath (DCLA, used with permission).

Sylvester, were buried in the church's graveyard, as was John Pollexfin, a man with whom Robert had financial dealings.

From the late sixteenth century, at least, the south side of the church was bounded by Kennedy's Lane, named for the builder of a row of ten houses on the south side of the lane (see p. 95 for a discussion of these houses). The house on the corner of Kennedy's Lane and St Nicholas Street evidently faced onto the lane. Richard Kennedy, in his 1679 articles, stated that he owned seven houses on St Nicholas Street. This matches the number of buildings shown on Rocque's 1756 map, as do the ten on Kennedy's Lane. It is hard to

Illus. 24—Photo of St Nicholas's church. Note the cobblestones; neighbouring buildings now flush (source unknown).

know whether any of the houses that Robert and Richard Kennedy caused to be built from the mid-seventeenth century survived into the eighteenth. Lack of maintenance appears to have been endemic in the city, and it seems that houses were torn down and rebuilt rather than repaired. Kennedy's Lane later disappeared in this process of destruction and construction. Another reason for the disappearance of much of the city's housing stock was the changing vision of what was desirable in terms of architectural fashion.

One last comment on St Nicholas Street is that it sloped down towards the location of St Nicholas Gate. This would have been located only 20 or 30ft north of where Bride Road currently meets St Nicholas Street. The street rose up from the level of the Poddle to the elevation of High Street and this slope is still visible today, though not much noticed by those in cars. Previously, it also curved slightly to the left going uphill, rather than today's curve to the right. The location of the

Market Cross at its High Street end ensured that St Nicholas Street was closely adjacent to much of the public activity in the city. All announcements, including marriage banns, would have been both proclaimed and posted there.

Illus. 25—The area of St Nicholas's church before local development (DCLA, used with permission).

Appendix E
Mount Kennedy in the seventeenth century

With the creation of the manor in 1664, the names of the townlands that became part of the demesne disappeared from sight. This primarily included Ballygarny, which was entirely eclipsed. Some, such as Cooladoyle and Ballyhorsey, lost major parts of their land area; others, such as Ballyronan and Kilquade, lost less. The Kennedys evidently built a tower-house on the motte, and later a grand house of seventeenth-century style, enlarged in the early 1670s. Warfare took a heavy toll on many of this century's buildings. The Kennedy tower-house, along with others in the area, was undermined during the 1641 rebellion. The grander house was at least damaged during the Williamite wars. It was, however, leased to Richard's widow in 1692, indicating that it was still habitable. The clearance of fields for tillage farming is documented for the 1630s. Animal grazing would have been the main agricultural activity for centuries before that.

The main road from Kilpedder to the new town would have followed the lane that today departs from the N11 and goes up towards the current mansion. In the seventeenth century it then ran towards the motte, curved around it to the right and descended to the river crossing, where today there is a bridge. It then continued down the current Church Road, making a straight path through what has become Newtownmountkennedy. Later, when privacy became more valued than control of the road, it was rerouted to travel east of the demesne, along the way it now takes to continue south.

The original settlement, most likely located to the west of the motte along the north side of the river, later became a range of outbuildings for the Kennedy farm. There were also houses for extended family members and for estate workers. There were orchards and gardens, a hop farm, fish-ponds, barns, stables, a malt-house, a mill, a pigeon-house, horse paddocks, a smithy, a tannery and various parks for wood. This list is primarily compiled from the lease given to Ann Barker Kennedy in 1692. It allowed her to keep some income from the estate after the death of her husband and their eldest son, the rent being less than the income from these productive resources.

When Robert Cunningham bought the manor in 1769 he began an extensive programme of landscaping, which would have substantially changed the layout of the demesne. It was during his time that the tower-house was removed. The stone from it and from the seventeenth-century mansion would most likely have been used to construct the mansion that now sits there, probably on the same site as the previous residence. To the extent that it can be determined, there is nothing left of any buildings from the seventeenth century.

If you would like to see the location of the motte, please go to https://maps.archaeology.ie/HistoricEnvironment/
zoom in to Mount Kennedy demesne in Co Wicklow, until you see 3 red dots on it. The one on the circular shape, marked 'mound' is the location of the motte. Click on the red dot. It will give you a catalogue number. Click on the arrow for information about the motte.

Appendix F
Signatures of major figures in the narrative

1 Robert Kennedy
2 William Parsons
3 William Rowlls
4 John Pue
5 George Sankey
6 Sankey Sulliard
7 Theobald Burke Baron of Brittas
8 John Kennedy
9 Adam Loftus
10 Robert Clony
11 Sylvester Kennedy
12 James O'Byrne
13 James Walsh
14 John Walsh
15 Walter Kennedy
16 James Carroll
17 Thomas Wentworth
18 George Radcliff
19 Farrell O'Cullen
20 Bernard Talbot
21 Humphrey Sulliard
22 John Hope
23 Richard Kennedy
24 Thomas Kennedy

25 *Ann [Barker] Kennedy*
26 *Robert Doyne*
27 *Robert Pue*
28 *John Parry, Bp of Ossory*
29 *Constance [Kennedy] Parry*
30 *Constance [Kennedy] Seymour*
31 *Edward Jones, Bp of Cloyne*
32 *Elizabeth Kennedy*
33 *Gilbert Heathcote*
34 *Sarah Kennedy*
35 *Sarah [Kennedy] Heathcote*
36 *Thomas Burdette*
37 *George Burdette*
38 *Ann Kennedy*
39 *Ann [Kennedy] Burdette*
40 *George Kennedy*
41 *Robert II Kennedy*
42 *Robert Hassells*
43 *Ralph Howard*
44 *Matthew Forde*
45 *Richard II Kennedy*
46 *Howard Kennedy*
47 *Katherine [Blake Kennedy] Howard*
48 *William Dudley*

Endnotes

Introduction

[1] Some of the others who similarly adapted were the Foxes in Offaly, some O'Farrells in Longford, O'Hara in Sligo, the MacGeoghans in Westmeath and, to some extent, the Walshes in Wicklow (Raymond Gillespie, pers. comm.).

[2] T.O. Ranger, 'Richard Boyle and the making of an Irish fortune, 1588–1614', *Irish Historical Studies*, vol. 10, no. 39 (1957), pp 257–97.

[3] Brid McGrath, pers. comm.

[4] David Edwards, 'The land-grabber's accomplices: Richard Boyle's Munster affinity, 1588–1603', in D. Edwards and C. Rynne (eds), *The Colonial World of Richard Boyle, First Earl of Cork* (Dublin, 2018), pp 166–88; see also David Edwards, 'Interrogating Richard Boyle: the Savoy House Proceedings of 1599', *Analecta Hibernica*, vol. 49 (2018), pp 79–115.

[5] Bernadette Cunningham, *Clanricard and Thomond, 1540–1640* (Dublin, 2012).

[6] Raymond Gillespie, 'A question of survival: the O'Farrells and Longford in the seventeenth century', in R. Gillespie and R. Moran (eds), *Longford: Essays in County History* (Dublin, 1991), pp 13–29; F. O'Ferrall, 'The downfall of the O'Ferralls of Mornine *c.* 1680–1789', in M. Morris and F. O'Ferrall (eds), *Longford: History and Society* (Dublin, 2010), pp 203–36.

[7] Bernadette Cunningham, 'Native culture and political change', in C. Brady and R. Gillespie (eds), *Natives and Newcomers* (Dublin, 1986), p. 158.

1. Making it in 'the Cittie'

[1] Colm Lennon, *The Lords of Dublin in the Age of the Reformation* (Dublin, 1989), p. 72; Kenneth Nicholls, pers. comm.

[2] NLI, GO MS 48, f. 24.

[3] G.E. Cokayne, *The Complete Baronetage*, vol. 4 (Exeter, 1900), pp 196–7 (accessed online; see Appendix A).

[4] *Calendar of the State Papers, relating to Ireland, of the reign of James I, 1603–1625* (ed. C.W. Russell and J.P. Prendergast), 1611–14, p. 111.

[5] The information about Dublin in the 1590s is taken from Colm Lennon's 'The great explosion in Dublin, 1597', *Dublin Historical Record*, vol. 42, no. 1 (1988), pp 7–22.

[6] L.J. Arnold, *The Restoration Land Settlement in Co. Dublin, 1660–1688* (Dublin,

1993), pp 16–17.

[7] Bernadette Cunningham, 'Native culture and political change', in C. Brady and R. Gillespie (eds), *Natives and Newcomers* (Dublin, 1986), pp 148, 152–4, 162.

[8] The information on the aldermen is found in Colm Lennon, 'Civic life and religion in early seventeenth century Dublin', *Archivium Hibernicum*, vol. 38 (1983), pp 14–25.

[9] 'June 1657: An Act for convicting, discovering and repressing of Popish Recusants', in *Acts and Ordinances of the Interregnum, 1642–1660*, ed. C.H Firth and R.S. Rait (London, 1911), pp 1170–80 (*British History Online*, http://www.british-history.ac.uk/no-series/acts-ordinances-interregnum/pp1170-1180; accessed 31 December 2021).

[10] Kai Erikson, *Everything in its Path* (New York, 1976), pp 153–4, as quoted in G. Hirschberger, 'Collective trauma and the social construction of meaning', *Frontiers in Psychology*, vol. 9, no. 1441 (2018), p. 3 (doi: 10.3389/fpsyg.2018.01441; accessed 31 December 2021).

[11] Judy Barry, 'James Carroll', *DIB*.

[12] NLI, Wicklow Papers, MS 38,638/2, 1632; they may or may not have been identifiably cousins, as it is a term also used between friends.

[13] *Encyclopaedia Britannica*, 'Puritanism' (https://www.britannica.com/topic/Puritanism; accessed 29 May 2021).

[14] T.O. Ranger, 'Richard Boyle and the making of an Irish fortune, 1588–1614', *Irish Historical Studies*, vol. 10, no. 39 (1957), p. 265.

[15] D. Edwards, 'The land-grabber's accomplices: Richard Boyle's Munster affinity, 1588–1603', in D. Edwards and C. Rynne (eds), *The Colonial World of Richard Boyle, First Earl of Cork* (Dublin, 2018), pp 173–5.

[16] Terry Clavin, 'William Parsons', *DIB*.

[17] B. Burke, *A Genealogical History of the Dormant, Abeyant, Forfeited and Extinct Peerages of the British Empire* (new edn) (London, 1866), p. 419, right column, lines 4–16, in *Wikipedia*, 'Sir William Parsons' (https://en.wikipedia.org/wiki/Sir_William_Parsons,_1st_Baronet_of_Bellamont; accessed 30 December 2020).

[18] Clavin, 'Parsons', *DIB*.

[19] *Calendar of Patent Rolls* (Dublin, *c.* 1830) [hereafter *CPR*], 17 James I, *xciv* 63 and 64, p. 465.

[20] J.T. Gilbert, *The History of the City of Dublin*, vol. 1 (Dublin, 1857), p. 11.

[21] NLI, Genealogical Office Manuscripts Collection: Funeral Entries (17 vols), vol. 7, p. 414.

[22] NLI, Wicklow Papers, MS 38,638/2, 27 November 1621; for this Exchequer role see G.E. Howard, *A Treatise of the Exchequer and Revenue of Ireland* (Dublin, 1776), pp 25–6 (https://archive.org/details/atreatiseexcheq00unkngoog/page/n106/mode/2up;_accessed 17 September 2021).

[23] Colm Kenny, 'The Four Courts at Christ Church 1608–1796', in W.N. Osborough (ed.), *Explorations in Law and History* (Dublin, 1995), pp 109–10.

[24] Howard, *A treatise*, pp 26–7.

[25] NAI, Ferguson Papers, vol. 2, pp 20–1. James Ferguson, who worked for the PRO in the nineteenth century, made notes from various record rolls concerning the Exchequer, here indicating the reimbursements due to the second

chamberlain of the Exchequer; the originals are no longer extant.

[26] NLI, Wicklow Papers, MS 38,640/7(3)1607.

[27] *Ibid.*, MS 38,638/13, 26 June 1609.

[28] *Ibid.*, MS 38,582/5, 10 October 1609.

[29] James Morrin (ed.), *Calendar of the Patent and Close Rolls of Chancery in Ireland, of the reign of Charles the First* (Dublin, 1863), p. 74.

[30] Mark Clinton, *Carrickmines Castle: Rise and Fall* (Dublin, 2019), p. 140; this surname is variously spelt 'Silyard' and 'Sulliard'.

[31] *The Complete Baronetage* (see Appendix A); dates are arrived at by the age of Sylvester's admission to Lincoln's Inns in 1630, assumed to be the usual fifteen years of age.

[32] J.T. Gilbert and R. Gilbert (eds), *Calendar of Ancient Records of Dublin* [hereafter *ARD*] (19 vols) (Dublin, 1889–1944), vol. 2, pp 253, 272; Andrew Somerville kindly clarified the nature of Sankey's service to Trinity.

[33] Henry VIII, Fiant no. 67; 'Pierce' is Anglo-Norman French for 'Peter'.

[34] NLI, GO MS, Funeral Entries, vol. 5, p. 7.

[34a] J.J. Goring, 'SULYARD, John (by 1518-75), of Wetherden, Suff.', in *The History of Parliament: The House of Commons 1509–1558*, ed. S.T. Bindoff, (London, 1982) (https://en.wikipedia.org/wiki/John_Sulyard; accessed 22 July 2022).

[35] Walter Fitzgerald, 'The Manor and Castle of Powerscourt', *Journal of the Co. Kildare Archaeological Society*, vol. 6 (1909–11), pp 126–39, Talbot family tree insert.

[36] NLI, GO MS, Funeral Entries, vol. 3, p. 90.

[37] *ARD*, vol. 2, pp 253, 272, 287, 329 and 443. George may possibly have been his son.

[38] NLI, GO MS, Funeral Entries, vol. 7, p. 414.

[39] *ARD*, vol. 3, pp 43, 235, 367, 438, 499, 501–2. He evidently died in 1659.

[40] NLI, Wicklow Papers, MS 38,571/2(2).

[41] *Ibid.*, MS 38,633/17(2); only the letters from Burke are extant, though Kennedy's response to the court charges is in the Wicklow Papers.

[42] *Ibid.*, MS 38,638/2, 13 September 1616.

[43] *Ibid.*, MS 38,566/2, 15 December 1615.

[44] *Ibid.*, MS 38,563/1(1).

[45] *Irish Builder and Engineer*, vol. 31 (Dublin, 1889), p. 113 (https://babel.hathitrust.org/cgi/pt?id=uiug.30112107848001&view=1up&seq=123; accessed 25 April 2021).

[46] The dark stone façade of this church can still be seen on Nicholas Street, just south of the Millennium Child Park on the corner with Christ Church Place. The street has been widened since the seventeenth century and it would have been located a few feet further out into what became the footpath. See Appendix D.

[47] James Hughes, *Patentee Officers in Ireland, 1173–1826* (Dublin, 1960).

[48] H. Wood, *Guide to Records Deposited in the Public Record Office of Ireland* (Dublin, 1919), p. 58:

'This office was appointed to register acts under 28 Henry VIII., c.19, by which the suing to Rome for licences, dispensations and faculties was abolished. The power to grant such faculties was given to the Lord Primate, but the faculty was made out by the Clerk of the Faculties in Chancery, upon receiving the confirmation of the Prerogative Court, and, after being sealed with the Great Seal, was registered by him. No records of this office have been transferred to the Public Record Office, but the Faculty Books in the Prerogative collection contain similar information. The office was amalgamated with that of Clerk of the Recognizances in 1858.'

[49] J. Byrne, *Byrne's Dictionary of Local History* (Cork, 2004), 'prerogative and faculties, court of the'. A benefice was the stipend given to a parish priest to provide him with a living.

[50] J. Mahaffy (ed.), *Calendar of State Papers relating to Ireland of the reign of Charles I [and Commonwealth] 1625–[1659]* (London, 1900–4) [hereafter *CSPI Charles I*], 1626, p. 159.

[51] L. Rowley (ed.), *Liber Munerum Publicorum Hiberniae* (London, 1824), Book 2, Part 2, p. 29.

[52] Grant of arms in 1618 to Robart Kennedy, from NLI GO MS 85, Draft Grants, *c.* 1630–1801, p. 83; I am grateful to Mark Clinton for drawing my attention to this event (http://catalogue.nli.ie/Record/vtls000511048#page/1/mode/1up).

[53] NLI, GO MS, Funeral Entries, vol. 4, p. 132.

[54] *Ibid.*, vol. 7, p. 53.

[55] *Ibid.*, vol. 16, p. 7.

[56] *Ibid.*, vol. 17, p. 217.

[57] NLI, Wicklow Papers, MS 38,638/22, 20 November 1618.

[58] *CPR* 17 James I, *xi* 20, p. 451.

[59] NLI, Wicklow Papers, MS 38,577/16(1).

[60] Lennon, *Lords of Dublin*, p. 237. There is no record of his having a brother by this name, and his son Thomas had not yet been born.

[61] NLI, Wicklow Papers, MS 38,638/2, 24 July 1620.

[62] *Ibid.*, MS 38,638/2, 22 December 1632.

[63] *Ibid.*, MS 38,640/7(3), 24 August 1625.

[64] Hughes, *Patentee Officers.*

[65] NLI, GO MS, Funeral Entries, vol. 7, p. 52.

[66] *Byrne's Dictionary*, 'remembrancer', p. 269, 'memoranda rolls', pp 195–6.

[67] Howard, *A treatise*, pp 13–14.

[68] *CSPI Charles I*, 1630, p. 534.

[69] NLI, Wicklow Papers, MS 38,638/11, 10 December 1609; MS 38,638/13, 26 June 1609; Colman's obligation to James Carroll may be another example of the buying of the pre-emption of this post.

[70] Deposition of Richard Northcrosse, 19 January 1642: 1641 Depositions, Trinity College Dublin, MS 811, ff 086r–086v (http://1641.tcd.ie/index.php/deposition/?depID=811086r058; accessed 8 November 2021).

[71] Depositions of Margarett Pont and Grace Pont, 24 March 1642: 1641 Depositions, Trinity College Dublin, MS 811, ff 083r–084v (http://1641.tcd.ie/index.php/deposition/?depID=811083r056; accessed 17 May 2020); Kenneth Nicholls brought this piece of information to my attention.

[72] *CPR* 22 James I, *lvi* 34, p. 575.

2. Expanding

[1] NLI, Wicklow Papers, MS 38,628/2, 14 July 1614; *CPR* 16 James I, *xxiii* 49, p. 365.

[2] *CPR* 19 James I, *cxl* 54, p. 513; also *x* 23, p. 515. This Thomas Cromwell was a descendant of Henry VIII's Thomas Cromwell; the younger man's father had moved to County Down in 1603 and inherited the title of 4th Baron Cromwell.

[3] John Ryan, *The History and Antiquities of Carlow* (Dublin, 1833), p. 159 (https://babel.hathitrust.org/cgi/pt?id=hvd.32044021647284&view=1up&seq=323&q1=Burdett; accessed 15 June 2021).

[4] NLI, Wicklow Papers, MS 38,628/2, 15 March 1627.

[5] L. Rowley (ed.), *Liber Munerum Publicorum Hiberniae* (London, 1824), Book 2, Part 2, pp 48, 82.

[6] *CPR* 17 James I, *xvii*, p. 445. The other burgesses were Sir Richard Masterson, Sir Edward Fisher, Colcott Chambre, Edmond Medhopp, William Plunkett and John Doyle.

[7] J. Byrne, *Byrne's Dictionary of Irish Local History* (Cork, 2004), 'burgess'.

[8] *CPR* 18 James I, *xv* 33, p. 468.

[9] Victor Treadwell, *An Investigation of the Irish Administration 1615–1622, and its Consequences, 1623–24* (Dublin, 2006), p. 661.

[10] G. Taylor and A. Skinner, *Maps of the Roads of Ireland* (London, 1783), p. 63; William Wilson, *The Post-Chaise Companion* (Dublin, 1805), p. 140 (references courtesy of Kenneth Nicholls).

[11] *CPR* 20 James I, *xii* 33, p. 552.

[12] NAI, D18351, D17562.

[13] NLI, Wicklow Papers, MS 38,582/5, 26 March 1622.

[14] *Ibid.*, MS 38,563/1(2).

[15] Mary was married in 1631. Assuming that she was around fifteen at the time, she would have been born in 1616.

[16] *CPR* 22 James I, *lvi* 34, p. 575.

[17] Christopher Maginn, *'Civilizing' Gaelic Leinster* (Dublin, 2005), pp 202–3.

[18] *CPR* 21 James I, *lii* 32 and *liii* 33, pp 574 and 575.

[19] T. Clavin, 'Gerald Comerford', *DIB* (https://www.dib.ie/).

[20] Geraldine Tallan, *Court of Claims* (Dublin, 2006), no. 211, pp 72–3.

[21] NLI, Wicklow Papers, MS 38,577/13(1).

[22] *Ibid.*, MS 38,566/2, 6 January 1625, 7 March 1625.

[23] *Ibid.*, MS 38,638/17, 10 June 1626.

[24] *Ibid.*, MS 38,577/4, 15 March 1682/3.

[25] Raymond Gillespie, 'Harvest crises in early seventeenth-century Ireland', *Irish Economic and Social History*, vol. 11 (1984), pp 10–11; 'Meal and money: the harvest crisis of 1621–4 and the Irish economy', in M. Crawford (ed.), *Famine: the Irish Experience 900–1900* (Edinburgh, 1989), pp 75–95.

[26] NLI, Wicklow Papers, MS 38,638/13, 1596; MS 38,639/3, 14 April 1600; MS 38,638/22, 19 June 1600; James Phillips often functioned as the clerk for these transactions.

[27] Kenneth Nicholls, pers. comm.

[28] NLI, Wicklow Papers, MS 38,582/1, 10 April 1622.

[29] *Ibid.*, MS 38,582/6(1), 24 March 1622/3.

[30] *Ibid.*, MS 38,638/12, 28 January 1621.
[31] *Ibid.*, MS 38,638/22, 20 March 1623.
[32] *Ibid.*, MS 38,639/3; 16 December 1623.
[33] *Ibid.*, MS 38,638/22, 15 April 1624. It also then required him to pay 'Harrington's rent' of £3+ going forward.
[34] *Ibid.*, MS 38,576/1, 18 April 1626; one third of Ballygarny, one eighth of Kilmurry (the area around the ruined church on Slaughter Hill), Cooladoyle (north of Easthill and west of the Mount Kennedy demesne), Drumbawn (the area north of the Hilltop Sports Club, running down to the Vartry River in the west), one third of Kilmacullagh (currently the east side of Newtown's main street, possibly the area now known as the townland of Newtown), Glanmoretagh (now the Altidore demesne) and Cloughentragh (not identifiable but probably part of Kilmurry).
[35] NLI, Wicklow Papers, MS 38,582/1, 20 March 1626. This portion is composed of Cooladoyle; half of the lands formerly owned by Keane O'Cullen in Killiskey parish, i.e. Ballinhorreh, Ballyliotts [these last two now Newtownboswell], Ballinehinch and Ballydoreen; two thirds of Ballygarny; one eighth of Kilmurry and Cloughentragh; Carriglough (the northern part of Tithewer, immediately south of Drumbawn down to the Vartry in the west); Drumbawn; Glanmoretagh [Altidore]; and three quarters of Kilmacullagh.
[36] *Ibid.*, MS 38,638/22, 21 March 1626/7.
[37] *Ibid.*, MS 38,582/16, 1 November 1633; MS 38,638/22, 1 May 1634; MS 38,638/22, 31 March 1636.
[38] *Ibid.*, MS 38,638/19, 28 March 1631.
[39] *Ibid.*, MS 38.638/15, 14 May 1631.
[40] *Ibid.*, MS 38,638/2, 27 November 1631.
[41] *Ibid.*, MS 38,638/22, 30 June 1636.
[42] These transactions are covered by dozens of the estate documents, as well as by one from the NAI. The purchases sometimes had to be first facilitated by transactions among the O'Byrnes to reconcile outstanding debts and agreements among themselves.
[43] NLI, MS GO Funeral Entries, vol. 7, p. 414.
[44] NLI, Wicklow Papers, MS 38,638/12, 10 September 1626.
[45] *Ibid.*, MS 38,566/4, 24 September 1627.
[46] *Ibid.*, MS 38,582/3(1), 1 October 1628.
[47] *Ibid.*, MS 38,638/2, 6 January 1628.
[48] TNA, Kew AO 1/280/1084, 9r; Raymond Gillespie, pers. comm.
[49] Edward Keane, P. Beryl Phair and Thomas U. Sadleir (eds), *King's Inns Admission Papers 1607–1867* (Dublin, 1982), p. 264.
[50] J.P. Mahaffy, *The Particular Book of Trinity College* (London, 1904), p. 241.
[51] J.P. Mahaffy, *An Epoch in Irish History* (London, 1903), pp 70–1.
[52] NLI, Wicklow Papers, MS 38,582/8(2), 19 May 1652, is the agreement between the Kennedys and Sylvester's wife, who was then a widow.
[53] Margaret Griffith, *Calendar of Inquisitions* (Dublin, 1991), pp 461, 462.
[54] Kenneth Nicholls, pers. comm. See also M. Clinton, *Carrickmines Castle: Rise and Fall* (Dublin, 2019), p. 81 and pp 286–8.
[55] B. Burke, *Burke's Irish Family Records* (Buckingham, 2007), p. 378, 'Doyne of Wells'.

[56] G.E. Cokayne, *The Complete Baronetage* (Exeter, 1900), vol. 5, pp 345–6.
[57] NLI, Wicklow Papers, MS 38,619/1(2).
[58] *Ibid.*, MS 38,638/2, December 1632.
[59] DCLA, Dublin Statute Staple, vol. 2, ID 1997, 12 November 1634.
[60] Clinton, *Carrickmines*, p. 139.
[61] NLI, Wicklow Papers, MS 38,638/22, 1 May 1634.
[62] TCD, Down Survey, map of Newcastle Barony, 1656 (see Illus. 10); John Lodge, Records of the Rolls, vol. 6, p. 488, 'The castle, towns, and lands of Ballygarne'.
[63] NLI, Wicklow Papers, MS 38,638/12, 1604.
[64] Muiris O'Sullivan and Liam Downey, 'Mottes', *Archaeology Ireland*, vol. 21, no. 1 (2007), pp 19–21; this information was brought to my attention by Rob Goodbody.
[65] Detail from *Hiberniae Regnum* (short title) by Nicholas Visscher II (1680), courtesy of RareMaps.com (https://www.raremaps.com/gallery/; accessed 17 January 2022).

3. Decades of turmoil

[1] Mark Empey, *Early Stuart Warrants* (Dublin, 2015), p. 187 (brought to my attention by Coleman Dennehy and Mark Empey).
[2] British Library, Egerton MS 2651, f. 109.
[3] NLI, Wicklow Papers, MSS 38,582/3(2); 38,582/4(2); 38,638/13, February 1636.
[4] *Ibid.*, MS 38,582/8(1).
[5] *Ibid.*, MS 38,582/7(3).
[6] A.B. Grosart (ed.), *The Lismore Papers of Richard Boyle, First and 'Great' Earl of Cork* (London, 1886), vol. 1, part 1, pp 259 and 270 (https://archive.org/details/lismorepapersri01corkgoog/page/n294/mode/2up?q=kennedy; accessed 30 April 2021).
[7] *Ibid.*, vol. 4, p. 170; see also pp 173–4, 197; vol. 3, pp 7, 16, 21, 122, 189, 191 and 196.
[8] James A. Culliton, 'City Hall Dublin', *Dublin Historical Record*, vol. 41, no. 1 (1987), pp 3–4; this information came to me via AnneMarie McInerney, Dublin City Librarian, and the citation via Ciaran Wallace.
[9] NLI, Wicklow Papers, MS 38,582/8(2).
[10] *Ibid.*, MS 38,622/7, December 1636.
[11] *Ibid.*, MS 38/622/7, November 1637.
[12] C. Lennon, *The Lords of Dublin in the Age of the Reformation* (Dublin, 1989), p. 237.
[13] NAI, Ferguson Papers, vol. 2, December 1637, p. 350.
[14] 'Paul Harris', *DIB*; cf. Thomas O'Connor, *Irish Jansenists 1600–1670* (Dublin, 2008).
[15] NLI, Wicklow Papers, MS 38,571/2(2), 4 May 1636.
[16] Representative Church Body Library, 'A Rent Roll of the Archbishop's Lands, 1682–1684', Clondalkin section, no. 114 of Miscellaneous Medieval Documents.
[17] NLI, Wicklow Papers, MS 38,571/2(2), 6 May 1636
[18] *Ibid.*, MS 38,622/7(3).

[19] John McCafferty, *The Reconstruction of the Church of Ireland: Bishop Bramhall and the Laudian Reforms, 1633–1641* (Cambridge, 2009), p. 56.

[20] NLI, Wicklow Papers, MS 38,619/1(3).

[21] *Ibid.*, MS 38,638/11 27 July/23 August 1639; MS 38,619/1(3).

[22] This position has been convincingly argued by Mark Empey; cf. 'The curious case of the lord deputy, the Carmelite, and the exorcised girl', in T. Dooley, M.A. Lyons and S. Ryan (eds), *The Historian as Detective: Uncovering Irish Pasts. Essays in honour of Raymond Gillespie* (Four Courts Press, 2021), p. 112.

[23] R.T. Kendall, *Calvin and English Calvinism to 1649* (Oxford, 1981) (https://en.wikipedia.org/wiki/History_of_the_Puritans_under_Elizabeth_I; accessed 13 January 2021).

[24] J.T. Gilbert, *The History of the City of Dublin* (Dublin, 1978 [1854]), vol. 1, p. 8.

[25] NLI, Wicklow Papers, MS 38,638/22, Cullen papers 5 July 1637.

[26] *Ibid.*, undated.

[27] NAI, Ferguson Papers, 2/446/5, vol. 2, p. 368.

[28] NLI, Wicklow Papers, MS 38,633/17(2).

[29] NAI, MS 2448 M[iscellaneous], pp 305–7.

[30] R. Gillespie, *Seventeenth Century Ireland* (Dublin, 2006), pp 79–82.

[31] TCD, 1641 Depositions Project, on-line transcript, January 1970 (http://1641.tcd.ie/deposition.php?depID<?php echo 809284r173?>; accessed 16 May 2020).

[32] *Ibid.* (http://1641.tcd.ie/deposition.php?depID<?php echo 811059r033?>; accessed 16 May 2020).

[33] *Ibid.* (http://1641.tcd.ie/deposition.php?depID<?php echo 811137r101A?>; accessed 16 May 2020).

[34] *Ibid.* (http://1641.tcd.ie/deposition.php?depID<?php echo 811164r119?>; accessed 16 May 2020).

[35] *Ibid.* (http://1641.tcd.ie/deposition.php?depID<?php echo 811055r030?>; accessed 16 May 2020).

[36] *Ibid.* (http://1641.tcd.ie/deposition.php?depID<?php echo 811132r097?>; accessed 16 May 2020); *ibid.* (http://1641.tcd.ie/deposition.php?depID<?php echo 811166r121?>; accessed 16 May 2020).

[37] *Ibid.* (http://1641.tcd.ie/deposition.php?depID<?php echo 811229r157?>; accessed 16 May 2020).

[38] DCLA, Dublin Statute Staple, vol. 2, ID 1129, 4 December 1622; vol. 2, ID 1316, 4 November 1625.

[39] W.J. Smyth, 'A cultural geography of the 1641 rising/rebellion', in M. Ó Siochrú and J. Ohlmeyer (eds), *Ireland, 1641: Contexts and Reactions* (Manchester, 2013), p. 87.

[40] Aidan Clarke, *The Old English in Ireland 1625–42* (London, 1966), pp 223–4.

[41] Gillespie, *Seventeenth Century Ireland*, p. 147.

[42] TCD, 1641 Depositions Project, on-line transcript, January 1970, County Wicklow, MS 811, ff 22–246 (https://1641.tcd.ie/index.php/browse/; accessed 16 May 2020).

[43] TCD, 1641 Depositions Project, on-line transcript, January 1970 (http://1641.tcd.ie/deposition.php?depID<?php echo 811070r044?>; accessed 16 May 2020).

[44] *Ibid.* (http://1641.tcd.ie/deposition.php?depID<?php echo 811166r121?>; ac-

cessed 16 May 2020).

[45] *Ibid.* (http://1641.tcd.ie/deposition.php?depID<?php echo 811169r123?>; accessed 16 May 2020).

[46] *Ibid.* (http://1641.tcd.ie/deposition.php?depID<?php echo 811225r155?>; accessed 16 May 2020); *ibid.* (http://1641.tcd.ie/deposition.php?depID<?php echo 811233r159?>; accessed 16 May 2020).

[47] *Ibid.* (http://1641.tcd.ie/deposition.php?depID<?php echo 811231r158?>; accessed 16 May 2020).

[48] C.W. Russell and J.P. Prendergast (eds), *The Carte Manuscripts in the Bodleian Library, Oxford: A report presented to the Right Honourable Lord Romilly, Master of the Rolls* (London, 1871), p. 166 (https://catalog.hathitrust.org/Record/100640335; accessed 29 May 2021). I am indebted to Paul Smith for this material.

[49] G. Tallan, *Court of Claims* (Dublin, 2006), no. 12, p. 5.

[50] NLI, Wicklow Papers, MS 38,567/1(1).

[51] G.E. Cokayne, *The Complete Baronetage* (5 vols) (Exeter, 1900) (https://archive.org/details/completebaroneta04coka/page/196/mode/2up?view=theater).

[52] J.T. Gilbert and R. Gilbert (eds), *Calendar of Ancient Records of Dublin* (19 vols) (Dublin, 1889–1944), vol. 3, p. 452; this would have involved a payment of 20*s*.

[53] G. Charles-Edwards, 'Calendar of petitions to Ormonde in 1649 and 1650', *Irish Genealogist*, vol. 6, no. 4 (1983), p. 440.

[54] Robert Mahaffy (ed.), *Calendar of the State Papers relating to Ireland preserved in the Public Record Office [Charles II] 1660–[1670]*, vol. 1, 1660–1662 (London, 1905), p. 100, 26 November 1660 (https://archive.org/details/cu31924091769566/page/n5/mode/2up; accessed 28 January 2022).

[55] Gillespie, *Seventeenth Century Ireland*, p. 184.

[56] R.C. Simington, *The Civil Survey of 1654–56: County of Dublin* (Dublin, 1996), p. 140.

[57] NLI, Wicklow Papers, MS 38,563/3 24 April 1652; 563/2.

[58] *Ibid.*, MS 38,582/8(2).

[59] NAI, RC 12/1, f. 98; the lands involved are: ¼ of Kilmurry Glencap, Templeglancap (both near the Downs), Ballymakandrick (Ballinahinch), ¼ of Ballyronan, Ballygarny, Cooladoyle, Carriglough, Kilmurry-Killinry, Knocknelough, Tithewer, Kilmacullagh, Monalin, Johnstown, Banog____ [*sic*] (a small portion of a townland), Moneycarroll, Mongflugh, Ballygarret, Drumbawn, Glanmoretagh and Kilpedder. I am indebted to Kenneth Nicholls for this document.

[60] J.C. Walsh, *The Lament for John MacWalter Walsh with Notes on the History of the Family of Walsh from 1170 to 1690* (New York, 1925), pp 241, 243, 245; *Carte* 44, fol. 583.

[61] Russell and Prendergast, *Carte Manuscripts*, 44, f. 583v; 42, f. 330.

[62] John Mahaffy (ed.), *Calendar of the State Papers relating to Ireland of the reign of Charles I [and Commonwealth] 1625–[1659]* (London, 1900–4), pp 616, 618, 834; 4 December 1656.

[63] Gilbert and Gilbert, *Ancient Records of Dublin*, vol. 4, p. 10.

4. Zenith

[1] Her mother was Sarah Norton (daughter of Bonham Norton); G.E. Cokayne, *The Complete Baronetage* (5 vols) (Exeter, 1900).
[2] Janet Kennish, *Datchet History* (http://datchethistory.org.uk/datchet-people/robert-barker/; accessed 3 January 2021).
[3] Raymond Gillespie, 'The changing structure of Irish agriculture in the seventeenth century', in M. Murphy and M. Stout (eds), *Agriculture and Settlement in Ireland* (Dublin, 2015), pp 125–7.
[4] NLI, Wicklow Papers, MS 38,582/6(1).
[5] *Ibid.*, MS 38,638/22, 31 March 1636.
[6] *Ibid.*, MS 38,577/2(1).
[7] *Ibid.*, MS 38,577/3(1).
[8] C.W. Russell and J.P. Prendergast (eds), *The Carte Manuscripts in the Bodleian Library, Oxford: A report presented to the Right Honourable Lord Romilly, Master of the Rolls* (London, 1871), Carte 44, f. 583v; Carte 42, f. 330.
[9] F.E. Ball, 'Sir Richard Kennedy', *Cork Historical and Archaeological Society Journal* (2nd ser.), vol. 8 (1902), p. 180. (For these references I am indebted to Hazel Maynard.)
[10] Edward Keane, P. Beryl Phair and Thomas Sadlier (eds), *King's Inns Admission Papers 1608–1867* (Dublin, 1982), p. 264.
[11] John Jubbes (1685), 'The Judges Opinions delivered before His Grace the Lord Chancellor of Ireland, in the cause between John St. Leger, Esq; plaintiff, and John Barret, Esq; defendant Taken by the register of the High Court of Chancery, Saturday the 8th of February, 1678. Present, Lord Chancellor, Lord Chief Justice Booth, Lord Chief Baron, Sir Richard Kennedy, Mr. Justice Johnson, Mr. Justice Jones, Sir Richard Reynell', *Early English Books Online Text Creation Partnership* (2011) (http://name.umdl.umich.edu/A70357.0001.001; accessed 29 May 2021).
[12] NLI, Wicklow Papers, MS 38,640/7(3).
[13] Simon Pender, *A Census of Ireland,* circa *1659* (Dublin, 2002), p. 363.
[14] NLI, Wicklow Papers, MS 38,639/20(2)17 December 1658.
[15] Aidan Clarke, *Prelude to Restoration Ireland* (Cambridge, 1999), p. 299.
[16] Scottish Record Office; R.P. Mahaffy (ed.), *Calendar of the State Papers relating to Ireland preserved in the Public Record Office [Charles II] 1660–[1670]* (London, 1905–10) [hereafter *CSPI Charles II*] (https://babel.hathitrust.org/cgi/pt?id=nyp.33433081633913&view=1up&seq=252&q1=Sir%20Richard%20Kennedy; accessed 12 May 2021).
[17] F.E. Ball, *The Judges of Ireland* (London, 1926), p. 347; this information was brought to my attention by Hazel Maynard.
[18] Clarke, *Prelude*, p. 206.
[19] Ball, 'Sir Richard Kennedy', p. 180.
[20] *Ibid.*, quoting Carte papers but giving no specific reference.
[21] J.T. Gilbert, *The History of the City of Dublin* (Dublin, 1854), vol. 1, p. 195. The listings in the Down Survey or the Books of Survey and Distribution may be where he got this information, though it could also be from documents since lost.
[22] NAI, Records of the Rolls: notes by John Lodge (15 vols), vol. 7, listings to 1677

in Charles II, p. 193.

23 NLI, Wicklow Papers, 38,567/1(2).

24 *Ibid.*, MS 38,638/2 1630 to 1664 bundle; MS 38,563/3 24 January 1662.

25 *Ibid.*, MS 38,615/15(1).

26 J.T. Gilbert and R. Gilbert (eds), *Calendar of Ancient Records of Dublin* (19 vols) (Dublin, 1889–1944), vol. 3, pp 308–9, 318, 320.

27 Ball, *Judges*, p. 347.

28 Russell and Prendergast, *The Carte Manuscripts*, p. 221 (https://babel.hathitrust.org/cgi/pt?id=uiug.30112001894135&view=1up&seq=229&q1=Sir%20Richard%20Kennedy; accessed 12 May 2021).

29 *Ibid.*, Carte 215, ff 189–90.

30 Edmond Gosse, *Jeremy Taylor* (London, 1904), p. 202; vol. 65 in J. Morely (ed.), *English Men of Letters* (https://babel.hathitrust.org/cgi/pt?id=chi.13591630&view=1up&seq=216; accessed 23 April 2021).

31 Paul G. Smith, 'Catholics and the Law in Restoration Ireland, 1660–1691' (unpublished Ph.D thesis, Trinity College Dublin, 2019); pers. comm.

32 Carte MS 215, ff 189–90.

33 Ball, *Judges*, pp 278–9.

34 Interestingly, Thomas Kennedy, Richard's younger brother, was made an under-register to the Land Settlement Commissioners. See *CSPI Charles II*, vol. 1, p. 278.

35 L.J. Arnold, *The Restoration Land Settlement in Co. Dublin, 1660–1688* (Dublin, 1993), p. 60, referencing the *Deputy Keeper's Report 19*, p. 64 (468).

36 Kenneth Nicholls, pers. comm.

37 Arnold, *Restoration*, p. 159

38 G. Taylor and A. Skinner, *Maps of the Roads of Ireland* (London, 1783), p. 63; William Wilson, *The Post-Chaise Companion* (Dublin, 1805), p. 140.

39 Kenneth Nicholls, pers. comm.

40 *CSPI Charles II*, p. 438.

41 *CSPI Charles II*, 1663–5, p. 438.

Ballygarny	Ballyvaughan [Ballyvolan?]
Cooladoyle	Glanmortagh [Glendarragh]
Tirahen [Tenysrath, Priestsnewtown]	Teetoore [Tithewer]
Drumbawn	Carricklough
Ballyhorsey	the two Carrigoures [Carriggower]
Moneflugh [part of Tithewer]	Ballironane ¼ [Ballyronan]
Killmurry Killinry [Kilmurry]	Balligarold [Ballygarret]
Monelen [Monalin]	Johnstown and Banagroe [an acre]
Kilmacollo [Kilmacullagh]	Ballinahensie [Ballinahinch]
Monecarrell [Moneycarroll]	Mulamea [Mullinaveige?, N of Roundwood]
Killpeder [Kilpedder]	Knocknesough [?]

42 These townlands are in Kilcoole parish: Killinpark, Downs, Drummin, East and West; in Lower Newcastle Parish: part of Killadreenan, Leamore, Upper and Lower; and in Killiskey parish: Ballydoreen, Newtownboswell (formerly Ballinhorreh, Ballyliotts), and Ballinahinch

43 Walter Harris, *The History and Antiquities of the City of Dublin, from the Earliest Ac-*

counts (Dublin, 1766), p. 76 (https://archive.org/details/b30517989/page/76/mode/2up; accessed 29 November 2021).

[44] NLI, Wicklow Papers, MS 38,577/4, 15 March 1682.

[45] *Ibid.*

[46] *Ibid.*, MS 38,563/7, 14 February 1679/80.

[47] Gilbert and Gilbert, *Ancient Records of Dublin*, vol. 3, pp 139, 315–16.

[48] NLI, Wicklow Papers, MS 38,563/5, 4 March 1675/6.

[49] Liam O'Rourke, pers. comm.

[50] 'John Parry', *Dictionary of National Biography, 1885–1900* (https://archive.org/details/dictionaryofnati43stepuoft/page/372/mode/2up; accessed 10 May 2021).

[51] W.M. Brady, in his *Clerical and Parochial Records of Cork, Cloyne, and Ross* (London, 1894), states that Sarah was Richard's eldest daughter, but her marriage year was around 1680. It would seem that Constance's marriage was lost sight of and has only come to light with this study of the Kennedy papers (https://archive.org/details/clericalandparo00bradgoog/page/n122/mode/2up?q=Heathcote; accessed 30 May 2021).

[52] NLI, Wicklow Papers, MS 38,563/ 5; MS 38,633/5(1).

[53] Liam O'Rourke, pers. comm.

[54] NLI, Wicklow Papers, MS 38,614/11(2); MS 38,566/6; MS 38,563/5; his next younger brother was born in 1634, so John would have been born before that.

[55] NLI, MS GO, Funeral Entries, vol. 4, p. 245.

[56] NLI, Wicklow Papers, MS 38,622/9, 18 November 1679; R.H. St Maur, *Annals of the Seymours* (London, 1902), p. 291 (https://babel.hathitrust.org/cgi/pt?id=nyp.33433081849840&view=1up&seq=417&q1=Sir%20Richard%20Kennedy; accessed 25 April 2021.

[57] Liam O'Rourke, pers. comm.

[58] D.L. Thomas, 'Jones, Edward (1641–1703)', *DNB, 1885–1900* (https://en.wikisource.org/wiki/Dictionary_of_National_Biography,_1885-1900/Jones,_Edward_(1641-1703); accessed 10 May 2021); cf. Brady, *Records of Cork, Cloyne, and Ross*, vol. 3, pp 102–3.

[59] Liam O'Rourke, pers. comm.

[60] NLI, Wicklow Papers, MS 38,577/15(2), 19 February 1679.

[61] Brady, *Records of Cork, Cloyne, and Ross*, vol. 2, p. 115. 'Nonconformity' would involve some connection with Protestant denominations outside the Church of Ireland.

[62] Thomas, 'Edward Jones', *DNB*; cf. Brady, *Records of Cork, Cloyne, and Ross*, vol. 2, pp 185–6; NLI, Wicklow Papers, MS 38,577/15(2), 19 February 1679.

[63] NLI, Wicklow Papers, MS 38,577/15(2), 19 February 1679.

[64] NLI, GO MS 207, Betham's 'Pedigrees', vol. 5, p. 187.

[65] NLI, GO MS 276. Because of its late date, however, it configures Sir Robt Kennedy, baronet, as the son of Robt Kennedy Chief Remembrancer, whereas they were in fact the same person. Further, perhaps taking their cue from Walter Kennedy's will, they list 'Patrick, Christopher, Markus, and George' as sons of the Remembrancer. Since there is no mention of them otherwise in this family, I think it is accurate to say that they are the sons of the alderman who were minors at the time their estate was bought (being listed as such in the al-

derman's will), and therefore became the legal sons of the Remembrancer.

[66] NLI, Wicklow Papers, MS 38,576/2, MS 38,574/3(2).

Courtfoyle	Callowhill
Kiltimon	Corsillagh & Ballybryne
Kilpatten (probably Kilpatrick/Kilquade)	Knockadreet
Ballybeg	Trudder
Carrignamuck	Ballyduff & Knockmill [?]
Kilfoyle [Kilfea?, part of Ballymaghroe]	Knockfadda
Keeloge	Timmore
Kilday	Knockballycargin [part of Knockadreet]
Ballynabarney	Ballyronan (the rest of it)

[67] Newcastle Parish Records (https://www.ireland.anglican.org/cmsfiles/pdf/AboutUs/library/AngRecord/Delgany/Delgany-Vol-1-03.pdf; accessed 23 June 2019).

[68] NLI, Wicklow Papers, MS 38,574/3(1); MS 38,576/4(1); MS 38,577/2(2).

[69] L. Rowley (ed.), *Liber Munerum Publicorum Hiberniae* (London, 1824), part 2, p. 62.

[70] M. Bence-Jones in his *A Guide to Irish Country Houses* (London, 1988), p. 215, states that the Mount Kennedy mansion was built in 1670 and was burned during the Williamite wars. Unfortunately, he gives no footnote for his assertion but only several pages of general bibliography, from which one would have to search individual titles to find the source for this.

[71] NLI, Wicklow Papers, MS 38,638/1, 1672.

[72] *Ibid.*, MS 38,582/17(2); MS 38,571/9; MS 38,582/17(1); MS 38,614/11(2).

[73] This exact document, dated 17 and 18 February 1679/80, has been lost, but MS 38,577/15(2), dated a day later, refers to it and summarises its contents.

[74] NLI, Wicklow Papers, MS 38,613/4(2).

[75] Great Britain, Public Record Office (1860–1939); *CSPI Charles II* (https://babel.hathitrust.org/cgi/pt?id=osu.32435018875013&view=1up&seq=597&q1=Sir%20Richard%20Kennedy; accessed 25 April 2021).

[76] NLI, Wicklow Papers, MS 38,566/7(2), 20 February 1676/7.

[77] *Ibid.*, MS 38,563/7, 14 February 1679/80.

[78] *Ibid.*, MS 38,577/15(2), 19 February 1679.

[79] *Ibid.*, MS 38,577/2(1).

[80] The Delgany church records also use the full name for a baptism (a Fanning) and a burial (a Parslie) in June and July of 1671 respectively.

[81] NLI, Wicklow Papers, MS 38,615/17.

[82] Henry F Berry, 'The water supply of ancient Dublin', *Journal of the Royal Society of Antiquaries of Ireland* (5th ser.), vol. 1, no. 7 (1891), pp 560–3.

[83] NLI, Wicklow Papers, MS 38,577/3(2).

[84] RCB Library, Register of the Church of St Nicholas Within (original MSS).

[85] John Bergin, 'Ralph Howard', *DIB.*

[86] NLI, Wicklow Papers, MS 613/4(1); the townlands involved are Kiltimon, Courtfoyle, Carrignamuck, Boleynass, Ballyronan, Knockraheen, Trudder, Keeloge, Timmore, Ballinahinch Upper and Lower, Upper Callowhill, Knockadreet and Knockatemple. This amounts to 6,000 acres, nearly half of the

Mount Kennedy estate.

[87] *Ibid.*, MS 38,613/4(2).

[88] *Ibid.*, MS 38,622/9(1) 28 November 1683.

[89] Delgany parish baptismal register.

5. Things fall apart

[1] Raymond Gillespie, *Seventeenth Century Ireland* (Dublin, 2006), p. 269.

[2] *Ibid.*, p. 252.

[3] NLI, Wicklow Papers, MS 38,577/17(1).

[4] *Ibid.*, MS 38,595/1, 10 May 1690.

[5] *Ibid.*, MS 38,595/1, 10 April 1688.

[6] Parish Register of the Church of St Nicholas Within.

[7] NLI, Wicklow Papers, MS 38,563/8.

[8] J.T. Gilbert, *The History of the City of Dublin* (3 vols) (Dublin, 1854), vol. 1, p. 194.

[9] *Irish Builder and Engineer*, vol. 31 (Dublin, 1889), p.128; (https://babel.hathitrust.org/cgi/pt?id=uiug.30112107848001&view=1up&seq=123; accessed 25 April 2021).

[10] NLI, Wicklow Papers, MS 38,563/8; information in the 'list of claims', dispensing property owned by William Kennedy, indicates that this property had belonged to Thomas Kennedy, not Richard. See NLI MS 3012, 'A list of the claims as they are entred [*sic*] with the Trustees at Chichester-House on College-Green Dublin, on or before the tenth of August, 1700' (Dublin, 1701), p. 6 (https://babel.hathitrust.org/cgi/pt?id=nyp.33433023122058&view=1up&seq=22&q1=Tho%20Kennedy; accessed 25 April 2021).

[11] NLI, Wicklow Papers, MS 38,615/15(3); only through the comparison of signatures has it been possible to determine that it was his sister rather than his mother who signed this document.

[12] *Ibid.*, MS 38,577/14(9).

[13] A. Allanson, *Biographies of English Benedictines* (Ampleforth, 1999), entry 499.

[14] NLI, Wicklow Papers, MS 38,577/15(2), 1685; John Walsh of Shanganagh had married Matthew's sister Jane Forde of Coolgreany, Co. Wexford, in the 1660s; see M. Clinton, *Carrickmines Castle: Rise and Fall* (Dublin, 2019), p. 277.

[15] NLI, Wicklow Papers, MS 38,577/15(2), 1688.

[16] *Ibid.*, MS 38,595/1.

[17] Manx National Heritage Archives, Parish Records, MS 09767/1/2, p. 121.

[18] NLI, Wicklow Papers, 38,595/1 10 April 1688.

[19] *Ibid.*, MS 38,599/9, 20 April, 1688.

[20] Douai Abbey, Weldon MS IV 74, 13 January 1692. I am indebted to Geoffrey Scott, OSB, Douai Abbey, Reading, UK, for his research into the life of William Kennedy as a Benedictine. He generously shared with me his knowledge, notes and relevant books.

[21] NLI, Wicklow Papers, MS 38,638/11, 30 May 1685.

[22] *Ibid.*, MS 38,599/9, 2 October 1688.

[23] *Ibid.*, MS 38,577/15(2), June 1689.

[24] Douai Abbey, Weldon MS IV 74, 13 January 1692.

[25] NLI, Wicklow Papers, MS 38,638/1, 26 November 1688.

[26] *Ibid.*, MS 38,595/12, undated list of expenses.
[27] *Ibid.*, MS 38,599/9, 4 December 1688.
[28] Allanson, *Biographies,* entry 499.
[29] NLI, Wicklow Papers, MS 38,624/1(2),12 June 1689.
[30] Trustees for the Sale of Forfeited Estates: Book of postings and sale of the forfeited and other estates, NLI MS LO LB 49 & 50, created in 1703 (reference courtesy of Paul G. Smith).
[31] NLI, Wicklow Papers, MS 38,599/8, 20 July 1714.
[32] *Ibid.*, MS 38,597/24(2), 4 January 1704.
[33] *Ibid.*,MS 38,597/24(2) 17 February 1704/5.
[34] *Ibid.*, MS 38,595/14(4); MS 38,574/15(2).
[35] Abbot Geoffrey Scott, pers. comm.
[36] Registry of Deeds, Book 10, pp 433–4, memorandum 4055.
[37] British Museum, Department of Manuscripts, and Humphrey Wanley, *A Catalogue of the Harleian Manuscripts in the British Museum. With Indexes of Persons, Places, and Matters* (London, 1808–12), p. 630 (https://babel.hathitrust.org/cgi/pt?id=gri.ark:/13960/t83j9rx1j&view=1up&seq=644&q1=Sir%20Richard%20Kennedy; accessed 25 April 2021).
[38] Weldon MSS, Annals of Douai Abbey, p. 74.
[39] NLI, Wicklow Papers, MS 38,638/1, 18 June 1713.
[40] PRONI, Rossmore Estate Papers, title document for Mount Kennedy, Co. Wicklow, from an official copy posted to me. Robert Cunningham, a Scotsman and a general in the army, was the next proper owner of the estate. It is the only document in those papers related to Mount Kennedy. Interestingly, this title document lists the elder Richard Kennedy as the first owner.
[41] Registry of Deeds, Dublin, Book 81, p. 40, no. 56020.
[42] Poole Papers: Hearth Money Rolls for Co Wicklow (1669), NLI MS 8818, Folder 6.
[43] 'A Memorial of an Indented Deed 4 April 1769 between Eliz Barker and Robt Cunningham' (MS in the possession of Elinor Nuttall Medlycott, Knockraheen, Newtownmountkennedy, Co. Wicklow, since donated to the NLI, to be filed with the Nuttall Papers). Most of what Elizabeth Barker got for the lease would have gone to repay the numerous interests that Robert Jones had given on the lease.
[44] Registry of Deeds, Book 59, p. 82, no. 39509, 13 May 1728; Book 68, p. 269, no. 47993, 14 March 1731; Book 71, p. 112, no. 49353, 21 June 1732; Book 81, p. 40, no. 56020, 30 May 1735.
[45] NLI, Wicklow Papers, MS 38,595/1, no date (1726?).
[46] PRONI, Rossmore Estate Papers, title document for Mount Kennedy, Co. Wicklow, from an official copy posted to me.

6. Tail-end

[1] G.E. Cokayne, *The Complete Baronetage* (5 vols) (Exeter, 1900), vol. 4, p. 197.
[2] Email from R. Athol, archivist of Lincoln's Inns, 11 April 2016. Their names were Danvers Hodges and Roger Mompesson.
[3] Janet Kennish, 'Datchet People': Robert Barker (http://datchethistory.org.uk/datchet-people/robert-barker/; accessed 3 Jan-

uary 2021).
[4] C.W. Russell and J.P. Prendergast (eds), *The Carte Manuscripts in the Bodleian Library, Oxford: A report presented to the Right Honourable Lord Romilly, Master of the Rolls* (London, 1871), MS 210/377.
[5] A. Allanson, *Biographies of English Benedictines* (Ampleforth, 1999), entry 499.
[6] Carte MS 210/376; other names used by Capt. Burk were Ld. Inniskillin, Sir Edward Fitzgerald, Capt. Brown, Coll. O'Neill and Esqr. Tirrall.
[7] Windsor, Royal Archives: Stuart Papers, 8 MAIN 168/164; from an electronic image.
[8] Personal communication from Geoffrey Scott, OSB, Ph.D, archivist for the English Benedictines.
[9] Royal Archives: Stuart Papers, 8 MAIN 168/164; from an electronic image.
[10] *Ibid.*, 8 MAIN 179, f. 4; from an electronic image.
[11] *Ibid.*, 8 MAIN 168/164; from an electronic image.
[12] *Ibid.*, 8 MAIN 169/4; from an electronic image.
[13] Allanson, *Biographies*, entry 499.

Appendix D

[1] Angret Simms, 'St Nicholas' churches in medieval Irish towns', in T. Dooley, M.A. Lyons and S. Ryan (eds), *The Historian as Detective: Uncovering Irish Pasts. Essays in honour of Raymond Gillespie* (Four Courts Press, 2021), pp 34–5.fgf

Bibliography

MANUSCRIPT PRIMARY SOURCES

National Archives of Ireland, Dublin

Betham, William: Abstracts of Prerogative Wills.

Ferguson Papers.

Miscellaneous Deeds, pre-1708, plantation grants.

Miscellaneous Documents.

RC 12/1, Record Commission: Repertories to Exchequer decrees, 1609, 1624–67.

Records of the Rolls: notes by John Lodge (15 vols).

National Library of Ireland, Dublin

Betham, William: Pedigrees, vol. 5, GO MS 207 and 276.

Genealogical Office Manuscripts Collection: Funeral Entries (17 vols).

Genealogical Office Manuscripts Collection: Draft Grants, *c.* 1630–1801, GO MS 85 (http://catalogue.nli.ie/Record/vtls000511048#page/1/mode/1up).

Nuttall Papers: 'A Memorial of an Indented Deed 4 April 1769 between Eliz Barker and Robt Cunningham'.

Poole Papers: MS 8818, Hearth Money Rolls for Co. Wicklow (1669).

Trustees for the Sale of Forfeited Estates: Book of postings and sale of the forfeited and other estates (1703), MS LO LB 49 & 50.

Trustees of Chichester House: 'A list of the claims as they are entred [*sic*] with the Trustees at Chichester-House on College-Green Dublin, on or before the tenth of August, 1700' (Dublin, 1701), MS 3012.

Wicklow Papers, of which the Mount Kennedy estate papers are a subset, MSS 38,521 to 38,640/7.

Dublin City Library and Archives
The Irish Statute Staple Books, 1596–1687 (3 vols).

Registry of Deeds, Dublin
Wills and Property Records.

Representative Church Body, Church of Ireland, Dublin
Miscellaneous Medieval Documents.
Parish Register of the Church of St Nicholas Within the Walls of Dublin.

United Kingdom
British Library, Egerton Papers, MS 2651, f. 109.
Douai Abbey, Reading, UK, Weldon MSS.
Kew TNA AO 1/280/1084, 9r.
Lincoln's Inns Archives
Manx National Heritage Archives: Parish Records, MS 09767/1/2.
Public Record Office of Northern Ireland: Rossmore Estate Papers.
Windsor, Royal Archives: Stuart Papers, MAIN/168, ff 181 and 164, MAIN/178, f. 110, MAIN/179, f. 4.

PRINTED PRIMARY SOURCES

Acts and Ordinances of the Interregnum, 1642–1660, ed. C.H. Firth and R.S. Rait (London, 1911).
Burke, B., *Burke's Irish Family Records* (Buckingham, 2007).
Calendar of the Patent and Close Rolls of Chancery in Ireland, of the reign of Charles the First, ed. J. Morrin (Dublin, 1863).
Calendar of Patent Rolls (Dublin, *c.* 1830).
Calendar of the State Papers, relating to Ireland, of the reign of James I, 1603–1625, ed. C.W. Russell and J.P. Prendergast (London, 1872–80).
Calendar of the State Papers relating to Ireland of the reign of Charles I [and Commonwealth] 1625–[1659], ed. J.P. Mahaffy (London, 1900–4).
Calendar of State Papers, 1660–1662, vol. 1, ed. R. Mahaffy (London, 1905) (https://archive.org/details/cu31924091769566/page/n5/mode/2up).
Calendar of the State Papers relating to Ireland preserved in the Public Record

Office [Charles II] 1660–[1670], ed. R.P. Mahaffy (London, 1905–10) (https://babel.hathitrust.org/cgi/pt?id=nyp.33433081633913&view=1up&seq=252&q1=Sir%20Richard%20Kennedy).

Calendar of State Papers relating to Ireland in the reign of Charles II: 1660–1688, ed. R.P. Mahaffy (London, 1910).

The Carte Manuscripts in the Bodleian Library, Oxford: A report presented to the Right Honourable Lord Romilly, Master of the Rolls, ed. C.W. Russell and J.P. Prendergast (London, 1871) (https://catalog.hathitrust.org/Record/100640335) (accessed 29 May 2021).

Clerical and Parochial Records of Cork, Cloyne, and Ross, ed. W.M. Brady (London, 1894) (https://archive.org/details/clericalandparo00bradgoog).

Cokayne, G.E., *The Complete Baronetage* (5 vols) (Exeter, 1900) (https://archive.org/details/completebaroneta04coka/page/196/mode/2up?view=theater).

Gilbert, J.T. and Gilbert, R. (eds), *Calendar of Ancient Records of Dublin* (19 vols) (Dublin, 1889–1944).

Grosart, A.B. (ed.), *The Lismore Papers of Richard Boyle, First and 'Great' Earl of Cork* (London, 1886) (https://archive.org/details/lismorepapersri01corkgoog/page/n294/mode/2up?q=kennedy).

Harleian Manuscripts, British Museum (https://babel.hathitrust.org/cgi/pt?id=gri.ark:/13960/t83j9rx1j&view=1up&seq=644&q1=Sir%20Richard%20Kennedy).

Jubbes, J., 'The Judges Opinions … by the register of the High Court of Chancery … 8th of February, 1678', *Early English Books Online Text Creation Partnership* (2011) (http://name.umdl.umich.edu/A70357.0001.001).

Mills, J. (ed.), *Registers of the Parish of St John the Evangelist, 1619–1699* (Dublin, 2000).

Newcastle [Co. Wicklow] Parish Records (https://www.ireland.anglican.org/cmsfiles/pdf/AboutUs/library/AngRecord/Delgany/Delgany-Vol-1-03.pdf).

Rowley, L. (ed.), *Liber Munerum Publicorum Hiberniae* (London, 1824).

Irish Manuscripts Commission

1641 Depositions (https://1641.tcd.ie/).

Empey, M., *Early Stuart Warrants* (2015).

Griffith, M., *Calendar of Inquisitions* (1991).

Hughes, J., *Patentee Officers in Ireland, 1173–1826* (1960).
Keane, E., Phair, P.B. and Sadleir, T.U. (eds), *King's Inns Admission Papers 1607–1867* (1982).
Pender, S., *A Census of Ireland,* circa *1659* (2002).
Simington, R.C., *The Civil Survey of 1654–56: County of Dublin* (1996).
Tallan, G., *Court of Claims* (2006).
Treadwell, V., *An Investigation of the Irish Administration 1615–1622, and its Consequences, 1623–24* (2006).

SECONDARY WORKS

Allanson, A., *Biographies of English Benedictines* (Ampleforth, 1999).
Arnold, L.J., *The Restoration Land Settlement in Co. Dublin, 1660–1688* (Dublin, 1993).
Ball, F.E., 'Sir Richard Kennedy', *Cork Historical and Archaeological Society Journal* (2nd ser.), vol. 8 (1902), pp 179–81.
Ball, F.E., *The Judges of Ireland* (London, 1926).
Barry, J., 'James Carroll', *DIB* (https://www.dib.ie/).
Bence-Jones, M., *A Guide to Irish Country Houses* (London, 1988).
Bergin, J., 'Ralph Howard', *DIB* (https://www.dib.ie/).
Berry, H.F., 'The water supply of ancient Dublin', *Journal of the Royal Society of Antiquaries of Ireland* (5th ser.), vol. 1, no. 7 (1891), pp 557–73.
Byrne, J., *Byrne's Dictionary of Irish Local History* (Cork, 2004).
Charles-Edwards, G., 'Calendar of petitions to Ormonde in 1649 and 1650', *Irish Genealogist,* vol. 6, no. 4 (1983), pp 423–44.
Clarke, A., *The Old English in Ireland 1625–42* (London, 1966).
Clarke, A., *Prelude to Restoration Ireland* (Cambridge, 1999).
Clavin, T., 'Gerald Comerford', *DIB* (https://www.dib.ie/).
Clavin, T., 'William Parsons', *DIB* (https://www.dib.ie/).
Clinton, M., *Carrickmines Castle: Rise and Fall* (Dublin, 2019).
Culliton, J.A., 'City Hall Dublin', *Dublin Historical Record,* vol. 41, no. 1 (1987), pp 2–15.
Cunningham, B., 'Native culture and political change', in C. Brady and R. Gillespie (eds), *Natives and Newcomers* (Dublin, 1986), pp 148–70.
Cunningham, B., *Clanricard and Thomond, 1540–1640* (Dublin, 2012).
Dictionary of Irish Biography (https://www.dib.ie/).
Dictionary of National Biography, 1885–1900 (https://archive.org/de-

tails/dictionaryofnati43stepuoft/page/372/mode/2up).

Edwards, D., 'The land-grabber's accomplices: Richard Boyle's Munster affinity, 1588–1603', in D. Edwards and C. Rynne (eds), *The Colonial World of Richard Boyle, First Earl of Cork* (Dublin, 2018), pp 166–88.

Edwards, D., 'Interrogating Richard Boyle: the Savoy House Proceedings of 1599', *Analecta Hibernica*, vol. 49 (2018), pp 79–115.

Empey, M., 'The curious case of the lord deputy, the Carmelite, and the exorcised girl', in T. Dooley, M.A. Lyons and S. Ryan (eds), *The Historian as Detective: Uncovering Irish Pasts. Essays in honour of Raymond Gillespie* (Four Courts Press, 2021), pp 110–13.

Erikson, K., *Everything in its Path* (New York, 1976).

Fitzgerald, W., 'The Manor and Castle of Powerscourt', *Journal of the Co. Kildare Archaeological Society*, vol. 6 (1909–11), pp 126–39.

Gilbert, J.T., *The History of the City of Dublin* (3 vols) (Dublin, 1854) (https://archive.org/details/historyofcityofd01gilb_0/page/n6/mode/2up?view=theater).

Gillespie, R., 'Harvest crises in early seventeenth-century Ireland', *Irish Economic and Social History*, vol. 11 (1984), pp 5–18.

Gillespie, R., 'Meal and money: the harvest crisis of 1621–4 and the Irish economy', in M. Crawford (ed.), *Famine: the Irish Experience 900–1900* (Edinburgh, 1989), pp 75–95.

Gillespie, R., 'A question of survival: the O'Farrells and Longford in the seventeenth century', in R. Gillespie and R. Moran (eds), *Longford: Essays in County History* (Dublin, 1991), pp 13–29.

Gillespie, R., *Seventeenth Century Ireland* (Dublin, 2006).

Gillespie, R., 'The changing structure of Irish agriculture in the seventeenth century', in M. Murphy and M. Stout (eds), *Agriculture and Settlement in Ireland* (Dublin, 2015), pp 119–38.

Goring, J.J., 'SULYARD, John (by 1518-75), of Wetherden, Suff.', in *The History of Parliament: The House of Commons 1509–1558*, ed. S.T. Bindoff, (London, 1982) (https://en.wikipedia.org/wiki/John_Sulyard; accessed 22 July 2022).

Gosse, E., *Jeremy Taylor* (London, 1904).

Harris, W., *The History and Antiquities of the City of Dublin, from the Earliest Accounts* (Dublin, 1766) (https://archive.org/details/b30517989/page/76/mode/2up).

Hirschberger, G., 'Collective trauma and the social construction of meaning', *Frontiers in Psychology*, vol. 9, no. 1441 (2018), pp 1–14 (doi: 10.3389/fpsyg.2018.01441).

Howard, G.E., *A Treatise of the Exchequer and Revenue of Ireland* (Dublin, 1776) (https://archive.org/details/atreatiseexcheq00unkn-goog/page/n106/mode/2up).

Irish Builder and Engineer, vol. 31 (Dublin, 1889) (https://babel.hathitrust.org/cgi/pt?id=uiug.30112107848001&view=1up&seq=123).

Kendall, R.T., *Calvin and English Calvinism to 1649* (Oxford, 1981) (https://en.wikipedia.org/wiki/History_of_the_Puritans_under_Elizabeth_I).

Kennish, J., *Datchet History* (http://datchethistory.org.uk/datchet-people/robert-barker/).

Kenny, C., 'The Four Courts at Christ Church 1608–1796', in W.N. Osborough (ed.), *Explorations in Law and History* (Dublin, 1995), pp 107–32.

Lennon, C., 'Civic life and religion in early seventeenth century Dublin', *Archivium Hibernicum*, vol. 38 (1983), pp 14–25.

Lennon, C., 'The great explosion in Dublin, 1597', *Dublin Historical Record*, vol. 42, no. 1 (1988), pp 7–22.

Lennon, C., *The Lords of Dublin in the Age of the Reformation* (Dublin, 1989).

McCafferty, J., *The Reconstruction of the Church of Ireland: Bishop Bramhall and the Laudian Reforms, 1633–1641* (Cambridge, 2009).

McCormack, A.M. and Clavin, T., 'Paul Harris', *DIB* (https://www.dib.ie/).

Maginn, C., *'Civilizing' Gaelic Leinster* (Dublin, 2005).

Mahaffy, J.P., *An Epoch in Irish History* (London, 1903).

Mahaffy, J.P., *The Particular Book of Trinity College* (London, 1904).

O'Connor, T., *Irish Jansenists 1600–1670* (Dublin, 2008).

O'Ferrall, F., 'The downfall of the O'Ferralls of Mornine *c.* 1680–1789', in M. Morris and F. O'Ferrall (eds), *Longford: History and Society* (Dublin, 2010), pp 203–36.

Ohlmeyer, J. and O Ciardha, E. (eds), *The Irish Statute Staple Books, 1596–1687.* Third supplement to *The Calendar of Ancient Records of Dublin* (ed. M. Clark) (Dublin, 1998).

Ranger, T.O., 'Richard Boyle and the making of an Irish fortune, 1588–1614', *Irish Historical Studies*, vol. 10, no. 39 (1957), pp 257–97.

Ryan, J., *The History and Antiquities of Carlow* (Dublin, 1833) (https://babel.hathitrust.org/cgi/pt?id=hvd.32044021647284&view=1up&seq=323&q1=Burdett).

Simms, A., 'St Nicholas' churches in medieval Irish towns', in T. Dooley, M.A. Lyons and S. Ryan (eds), *The Historian as Detective: Uncovering Irish Pasts. Essays in honour of Raymond Gillespie* (Four Courts Press, 2021), pp 34–6.

Smith, P.G., 'Catholics and the Law in Restoration Ireland, 1660–1691', (unpublished Ph.D thesis, Trinity College Dublin, 2019).

Smyth, W.J., *Map-Making, Landscapes and Memory: A Geography of Colonial and Early Modern Ireland* c. *1530–1750* (Cork, 2008).

Smyth, W.J., 'A cultural geography of the 1641 rising/rebellion', in M. Ó Siochrú and J. Ohlmeyer (eds), *Ireland, 1641: Contexts and Reactions* (Manchester, 2013), pp 71–94.

St Maur, R.H., *Annals of the Seymours* (London, 1902) (https://babel.hathitrust.org/cgi/pt?id=nyp.33433081849840&view=1up&seq=417&q1=Sir%20Richard%20Kennedy).

Taylor, G. and Skinner, A., *Maps of the Roads of Ireland* (London, 1783).

Walsh, J.C., *The Lament for John MacWalter Walsh with Notes on the History of the Family of Walsh from 1170 to 1690* (New York, 1925) (https://babel.hathitrust.org/cgi/pt?id=mdp.39015025923155&view=1up&seq=7).

Wilson, W., *The Post-Chaise Companion* (Dublin, 1805).

Wood, H., *Guide to Records Deposited in the Public Record Office of Ireland* (Dublin, 1919) (https://www.nationalarchives.ie/wp-content/uploads/2019/03/Herbert-Woods-Guide-to-Public-Records_2_Part1.pdf).

Index